crowd breakers & MIXERS

THE ideas LIBRARY

FOR YOUTH GROUPS

THE IDEAS LIBRARY

crowd breakers & MIXERS

THE ideas LIBRARY

FOR YOUTH GROUPS

Youth Specialties

ZondervanPublishingHouse
Grand Rapids, Michigan
A Division of HarperCollinsPublishers

Project editor: Vicki Newby
Cover and interior design: Curt Sell
Art director: Mark Rayburn

ISBN 0-310-22037-8

Printed in the United States of America

98 99 00 01 02 03 04 05 06/ /10 9 8 7 6 5 4 3

CONTENTS

So what killer crowd breaker have you invented lately?

Are your kids still talking about that mixer you invented for last month's meeting or party? Youth Specialties pays $25 (and in some cases, more) for unpublished, field-tested ideas that have worked for you.

You've probably been in youth work long enough to realize that sanitary, theoretical, tidy ideas aren't what in-the-trenches youth workers are looking for. They want—*you* want—imagination and take-'em-by-surprise novelty in meetings, parties, and other events. Ideas that have been tested and tempered and improved in the very real, very adolescent world you work in.

So here's what to do:

• Sit down at your computer, get your killer crowd breaker out of your head and onto your hard drive, then e-mail it to ideas@youthspecialties.com. Or print it off and fax it to 619-440-4939 (Attn: Ideas).

• If you need to include diagrams, photos, art, or samples that help explain your crowd breaker, stick it all in an envelope and mail it to our street address: Ideas, 1224 Greenfield Dr., El Cajon, CA 92021-3399.

• Be sure to include your name and all your addresses and numbers.

• Let us have about three months to give your idea a thumbs up or down*, and a little longer for your 25 bucks.

*Hey, no offense intended if your idea isn't accepted. It's just that our fussy Ideas Library editor has these *really* meticulous standards. If the crowd breaker isn't creative, original, and just plain fun in an utterly wild or delightful way, she'll reject it (reluctantly, though, because she has a tender heart). Sorry. But we figure you deserve only the best ideas.

GAGS AND
SKITS

These loosen up an audience vicariously, for they require the active participation of only a few kids at most—up front, or onstage. These gags and skits generally involve a short set-up and a humorous pay-off—often at the expense of an unwitting but good-natured "victim." (For a vast collection of skits, many of which can be adapted for use as crowd breakers, see *Drama, Skits, & Sketches* in the Ideas Library.)

BUCKET TRICK

Before your kids arrive, half fill a bucket with confetti or rice. Carefully place a ladle filled with water on top of the rice, making sure that no water gets spilled and that the ladle remains dry on the underside. Cover the top of the bucket to hide its contents. After everyone arrives and is gathered around (not too close), announce that you have acquired water from the fountain of youth. Carefully remove the ladle without spilling the water or revealing the contents of the bucket. Then pour the water from the ladle into a glass and have a volunteer (an accomplice) drink it. After a brief pause, the volunteer should start acting like a toddler. Then he or she should grab the bucket and throw its contents on the group. Surprise! It's just rice, not water.

BASKETBALL AWARDS

The following awards can be presented to members of the school or church basketball team at a "fifth quarter" social event, or youth meeting. The tro-phies can be mounted on wooden bases and the plaques on 6x12-inch pieces of plywood. All should be sanded, varnished, and made to look as much like the real thing as possible. Names can be done with a plastic label-making device.

• **Player with the greatest offense.** Bottle of mouth-wash on a base.
• **Player who smiles the most.** Tube of toothpaste on a plaque.
• **Player with the most fouls.** A chicken (dead or alive) or free dinner at Kentucky Fried Chicken.
• **Most energetic player.** Vitamin pill on a base.
• Best substitute player: Book to read while sitting on the bench.
• **Toughest player.** Bottle of Brut aftershave on a base.
• **Most injured player.** First-aid kit on a base.
• **Player with most baskets.** Easter basket full of candy eggs.
• **Best dribbler.** Baby bib on a plaque.
• **Best jumper.** Frog (real or phony) on a base.
• **Best "clutch" player.** Old clutch or brake pedal on a base.

You can add more to this list with a little creativity. Serious trophies or awards to outstanding players can also be added to end on a positive note.

Ron Allchin

BUZZ, BUZZ, LITTLE BEE

Make everyone a little uneasy by announcing that you are going to give a lesson on the birds and the bees. Point out that due to a lack of time you will cover only the bees part now.

Next, select a player from the group who's a good sport and who will play along enthusiastically. Seat the player in a chair in front of the group. The player is to pretend that the room is a garden, that the stage area is the beehive, and that he is the queen bee, the ruler of the hive. Explain that you are the worker bee. Your job is to gather pollen from the garden and bring it back to the hive. Each time you return to the beehive with your load of pollen, you will say (in bee language), "Whompf!" (Explain that you will gather a larger load of pollen each time you go out, making it more difficult for you to speak each time you return.) Then the queen bee must reply, "Buzz, buzz, little bee. Give it all to me." Practice this scenario a few times with the player and have the group applaud.

When you go out into the garden, flap your arms and buzz a lot to make it fun to watch. Make sure that on each flight you find a spot that is out of sight of the player, behind a screen, for example. On your third or final flight, fill your mouth with water while you are out of sight, return to the queen bee, and say "Whompf!" After the queen bee replies, spit your water all over him.

You may or may not want the audience to see that you have filled your mouth with water on your final flight. Either way will add to the fun. Or fool the audience and ensure the stunt's success by having the volunteer be an accomplice who pretends to be shocked or mad in the end.

DOOR SUR-PRIZES

Give away a door prize at every party. Here are some suggestions:
- **The Perfect Gift to Take Care of All Your Hang-Ups.** Two clothes hangers. Also keeps your room clean.
- **Fourteen-Carrot Gold Ring.** Fourteen carrots with greens secured together in a giant ring, sprayed with gold paint. Hang around winner's neck.
- **California Wet Suit.** One pair of baby's plastic pants. A vacation must. Stops the water, but not the sun.
- **Tickets to a Free Dinner.** Give two blank tickets. Dinner follows the floor show which begins at 7:30. Courtesy of the San Francisco (or any glamorous city) Gospel Mission.
- **Motorized Brick for Lazy Radicals.** Attach wings, engine, and propeller from an inexpensive toy plane to a brick. Eliminates effort, personal involvement, and risk of incarceration. Just aim brick on a long, smooth surface and start the engine.
- **A Couple of Dates Lined Up for Two Guys.** Two attractive girls come out, hold up a long string threaded through two dates (fruit).
- **Free Chicken Dinner.** One small plastic bag full of birdseed, a dinner to delight any chicken.
- **Automatic Egg Beater.** Tell your students, "We couldn't afford the giant-sized maxi-stir or the medium-sized midi-stir, so we are giving you the inexpensive mini-stir. Pastor Jones, would you please say a few words appropriate for the occasion?" The pastor could respond with the following: "When the time's up, just pull my plug. Actually, Joe's afraid I'll get you all mixed up."
- **Vacuum Cleaner or Dishwasher.** Introduce the surprise clean-up committee or K. P. crew to be run by the winner.

Dave Cassel

FORTUNE-TELLER

Select a trusted adult who is unfamiliar to your kids to help you with this activity. Announce that your adult guest has supernatural powers. He or she can tell strangers about their pasts and predict their futures. Act as if you are randomly choosing two or three kids and invite your guest to describe bits of humorous (but true) information about the subjects. Of course, you have secretly gathered this information ahead of time from parents and briefed your guest with it. After you have had some fun with this, clue the audience in. You can use this activity along with a session on Scripture's perspective on fortune-telling.

GURU, THE MIND READER

This stunt is good for small casual meetings or at socials. All that is needed is a telephone. You announce to the group that there is a "guru" in town, whom you can call anytime and ask to name any card (from a regular deck of cards) that you have chosen ahead of time. He will always name the right card on the first guess. To prove this, have the group choose a card (eight of spades, for example). You then call the guru, who is actually someone clued in ahead of time, waiting for your call. When he answers, he immediately starts counting, "Two, three, four, five, six" and when he reaches the right number or name (queen, king, ace) of the card, you say, "Hello, may I speak to the guru, please?" The guru then names the suits (clubs, hearts, spades, diamonds). As soon as he names the correct one, you interrupt with "Hello, guru, we have chosen a card we would like you to guess." Put one of the kids on the line to listen as he names the card, much to the amazement of all. *David Parke*

LETTER FROM GRANDMA

On page 16 is a fun letter that can be read for laughs. Read it slowly and pause after each period. If you use it at a camp, you can read it during mail call. Just introduce it by explaining, "There wasn't a name on the envelope, and we couldn't figure out who this letter was to. Maybe you will recognize it if we read it. It's from your grandma. . . ." *Eugene Gross*

MOUTHWASH SALES REPS

This is a good stunt for a rally-type youth meeting when it would be possible to send two or three kids out on the street for a period of 20 to 30 minutes at the start of the meeting and then return with results. The idea is to test their sales ability with a ridiculous product, namely reclaimed mouthwash. Two kids are given the props described in the sales pitch below and are given a certain length of time to go door-to-door to try to sell the product. An assistant goes with each of them to keep score on how well they do. The participants are given a copy of the sales pitch on page 17 (read it to your audience before the kids leave), and each kid must read it to the people who answer the door and go through all the motions described. (Use colored water for mouthwash and a radio speaker as a breath meter.)

The scoring is as follows: If the customer buys the mouthwash, the sales rep gets 2000 points. If the customer tries the mouthwash, the sales rep gets 1000 points. If the sales rep can get all the way through the whole pitch without laughing or getting the door slammed in his face, he gets 500 points. At the end of the time limit, the sales reps return to the meeting and the one with the highest score is the winner.

PARK BENCH

Send three or four people, either boys or girls, out of the room. While they are out, have a boy and girl sit side-by-side on a park bench (or two chairs). Bring in one of the people waiting outside the room. Tell her that the people on the park bench like each other a lot, have just been out on a date, and continue to give a big build-up. Then ask her to arrange the two people in a position to make them look more romantic (such as holding hands or embracing). The fun begins when, after doing this, she must take the place of the girl, doing what she suggested. Bring in the next person and repeat the process. Continue until you feel it is time to stop. *Lynne Surft*

PASTOR SPLICE

First obtain cassette recordings of several of your pastor's sermons. Then use two tape recorders (or a dual

Dear Sonny,

Since I have time because I am not busy, I thought I would write you a few lines and let you know the up-to-date news. We are all as well as can be expected, for the condition we are in. We ain't sick, we just don't feel good. I am feeling fine; Aunt Martha is dead. I hope this letter finds you the same. I suppose you will want to hear about us moving from Illinois to Hollywood. We never started until we left. It didn't take us any longer than from the time we started until the time we arrived. The trip was the best part of all. If you ever come out here, don't miss that.

They didn't expect to see us until we arrived, and most of the people we were acquainted with, we knew, and the people we didn't know seemed like strangers. We still live at the same place we moved to last, which is beside our nearest neighbors across the road from the other side. Randy says he thinks we will stay here until we move or go somewhere else.

We are very busy farming. Eggs are a good price; that's the reason they are so high. Some of the ground here is so poor you can't raise an umbrella on it, but we have a fine crop of potatoes. Some of them are the size of a hickory nut, some the size of a pea, and then there are a whole lot of little ones.

Pete was taking the cows to water and when they went across the bridge, one fell through and strained her milk. Now she has the hiccups once a week and churns her own butter.

Sharon fell through the back porch. It bruised her somewhat and skinned her elsewhere.

Every time Bill gets sick, he starts feeling bad. The doctor gave him some medicine and said if he got better it might help him, and if he didn't get any worse, he would stay about the same.

I would have sent you the five dollars I owe you, but I already had this letter sealed before I thought of it. I sent your overcoat, but I cut the buttons off so it wouldn't be so heavy. You can find them in the left-hand pocket.

We were out of jelly, so Bob went to New York to get some of the traffic jam. Well, I think I must close now. It took me three days to write this letter because you are a slow reader.

All my love,

Grandma

P. S. We now live in Hollywood where everything is modern. We have a kitchen, living room, dining room, and two bedrooms. And then there is one little room upstairs to water the horses out of, only more fancy. Then there is a little white thing about three feet tall with hot and cold water. It wasn't any good, though, 'cause there was a hole in it. Then there is another thing over in the corner that is the handiest thing in the house. You can put one foot down in it and wash it all over and press a little lever and you can have clean water for the other foot. It has two lids on it. We took the solid lid off and we roll pie dough on it, and the other lid had a hole in it, so we framed Grandpa's picture in it. Everybody said it looked just as natural as if he were sitting there.

The Sales Pitch

Hello, I represent _____ and we would like you to take just 60
name of your group
seconds of your time to participate in our community hygiene survey. It consists
of four simple questions:

1. Have you visited your dentist this year?

2. Would you say you and your family brush seldom, usually, or always?

3. Which brand of mouthwash do you prefer?

4. Would you repeat slowly the words "Hello, Happy, Harry" into this simple
breath meter?

   I appreciate your cooperation in this test, and just before I go I would like to
call your attention to a new product that we feel will revolutionize the mouth
hygiene industry. By an amazing scientific process, we have found a way to
reclaim used mouthwash. It will soon be on sale in your local drug store, but during our introductory door-to-door advertising campaign, I am able to offer you an
entire gallon of reclaimed mouthwash at the astounding price of just one dollar.
That's quite a bargain, isn't it? (*Get response.*) I'm sure you'll want to take advan-
tage of this offer tonight. I am authorized to leave this giant economy gallon
with you for only one dollar. Would you like me to step in or wait here while
you get your money? (If the person buys, thank him or her and go on. In the
answer is no, continue).

   I understand your feeling about buying a new product, but there is one more
thing I'm sure you will be delighted to do. Here is a small sample of our
reclaimed mouthwash. Would you agree to try it and give me your reaction to
the product? Just take the bottle and put a small amount in your mouth and
rinse thoroughly. Then deposit the mouthwash back into the bottle through this
funnel. I think this demonstration alone will show you the distinct advantages of
reclaiming mouthwash.

cassette recorder) to edit phrases of the pastor's sermons as answers to your own contrived questions. You can then play an authentic interview of the pastor with some rather hilarious results.

Here's a sample:

Interviewer: Describe your boy, Peter, in two words.

Pastor: Behavioral problem.

Interviewer: How about your other son, Dave?

Pastor: Lazy and weak.

Rick Porter

THE W.C.

This is a crowd breaker that is simply read to the group. Give the following background information.

While vacationing in Switzerland, a British woman decided that she wanted to live there. But first she needed to find a room to rent. She asked the schoolmaster in the local town to recommend a room. He took her to see several of them. When everything was settled, the woman returned to Britain to make final preparations to move. When she arrived home, however, the thought occurred to her that she had not seen a "W.C." in the place she had rented. (A W.C. is a water closet or a bathroom.)

So she immediately wrote a note to the schoolmaster asking him if there was a W.C. in the place. The schoolmaster did not know what W.C. meant, so he asked a local priest if he knew what it meant. Together they tried to find the meaning of the letters W.C. They finally decided that it could only mean "wayside chapel" or a small chapel alongside a country road. The schoolmaster then wrote the following letter to the British woman:

(Read the letter on page 19.)

My Dear Madam,

I take great pleasure in informing you that the W.C. is situated nine miles from the house in the center of a beautiful grove of pine trees surrounded by lovely grounds.

It is capable of holding 229 people, and it is open on Sundays and Thursdays only. As there are a great number of people expected during the summer months, I suggest that you arrive early, although usually there is plenty of standing room. This is an unfortunate situation, especially if you are in the habit of going regularly. It may be of some interest to know that my daughter was married in the W.C., and it was there that she met her husband. I can remember the rush there was for seats. There were three people to every seat usually occupied by one. It was wonderful to see the expressions on their faces.

You will be glad to hear that a good number of people bring their lunch and make a day of it, while those who can afford to go by car arrive just on time. I would especially recommend that your ladyship go on Thursdays when there is an organ accompaniment. The acoustics are excellent, and even the most delicate sounds can be heard everywhere.

The newest addition is a bell donated by a wealthy resident of the district. It rings each time a person enters. A bazaar is to be held to provide for plush seats for all, since the people feel it is long needed. My wife is rather delicate so she cannot attend regularly. It is almost a year since she went last, and naturally it pains her very much not to be able to go more often.

I shall be delighted to reserve the best seat for you, where you shall be seen by all. For the children, there is a special day and time so that they do not disturb the elders.

Hoping to be of some service to you,

The Schoolmaster

These go a long way toward alleviating the awkwardness of self-conscious kids forced to introduce themselves to each other. Some of these mixers are creative ways to learn each other's names. Others offer nonthreatening opportunities for interaction that allow kids to discover more about each other.

BOGGLE MIXER

Divide your young people into small groups. Each member of the small group writes their first name in large letters on a single piece of paper in a vertical list with a uniform left margin.

Each group then tries to make as many words as possible (three letters or more) from the combined letters of the names. Any combination can be used as long as the letters are contiguous in any direction. Give one point for three- and four-letter words. Give two points for five-letter words and three points for six-letter words. Proper names and foreign words are not permissible. Set a three-minute time limit. *Gary K. Sturni*

CAREER GUESS

If you're planning a career night with your youth group, try this as an icebreaker. Put up a large sheet of newsprint or paper for each person present. If you don't have enough wall space, tape the sheets to the tops of tables. Write a different person's name at the top of each sheet, and give everybody a marker.

Participants go to every sheet except their own and write the occupations that they think the others will have after they finish their education. Any criteria is okay. After everyone is finished, students write their own projected careers on their sheets. *Marja Coons*

CHAIN REACTION

Prepare 8½x11-inch sheets of paper, each with a different question at the top. The questions may come from the following list or from your own collection.

- What is the most enjoyable part of the day for you?
- What would you consider to be your greatest accomplishment?
- What is it about you that your mother or father brags about the most?
- Which TV show do you watch the most?
- Have you ever played a musical instrument?
- Do you know any good jokes? Tell me one.
- What do you like about school?
- Where have you been that no one else in the room has been?
- What is the most beautiful thing you have?
- What is your favorite seasonal activity?
- Where were you born?
- What were you last Halloween?
- What is your favorite book?
- Where is your favorite place to eat?
- What percentage of the Bible would you say you have read?
- What is your motto for your life?

The question on every paper is marked with the number 1. Now follow these steps to create your own chain reaction:

1. Everyone mingles and pairs up. Students ask their partners the one question from their own sheets. They needn't write down the answer—just listen.

2. Then students copy their partners' questions to their own sheets and number it 2.

3. Now everyone mingles again and finds new partners. Students ask their new partners the new question they just copied onto their sheets from the latest partner.

4. They listen to the answers, then copy their new partners' question 1 to their own sheets and label it 3.

Continue until students have thoroughly mingled or set a time limit.

Always ask the last question on the list, and always copy the first question. *John Morgan*

CHARACTER ANALYSIS

When members of a group don't know each other very well, have everyone write down some information about themselves on a sheet of paper, without their names. Information could include the following:

- Favorite food
- Middle name
- Hobby

- Favorite TV show
- Most embarrassing moment

Have the kids pass them in. They are shuffled and redistributed. Students read their slips of paper to the rest of the group one at a time. The group then tries to guess who the person is from the information. This is a fun way to have kids get better acquainted. *Roger Paige*

CONNECT-A-NAME

This get-acquainted activity uses only a large piece of paper and a felt-tip marker. Form teams of four to six people each. For round one, at a signal each team attempts to connect every team member's first name in one crossword puzzle (see diagram) in the

```
KYLE
E
EVA
I      )
NELLIE
L
LANCE
```

shortest amount of time. For round two combine two teams and play it again. Continue playing rounds until all are in one big team and making a crossword puzzle of all the names. You can display the final crossword during a Bible study on 1 Corinthians 12 to illustrate that all Christians are part of the same body. *Michael W. Capps*

COMMON GROUND

This is a fun small group experience that helps teens get to know each other better. Divide into small groups of five to seven and distribute the list on page 26, one to each group. Assign someone in each group to be the recorder. The basic idea is for each group to come up with something that they *all* like and *all* dislike in a variety of categories. They are encouraged to be honest rather than just trying to go for the points.

For each consensus reached, the group will

receive a certain number of points (you decide). You could give 10 points for any answer that everyone in the group has in common, and fewer points for answers that only some of the kids in the group have in common. For example, if only five out of the group of seven have a particular thing in common, then they would get only five points instead of 10. Set a time limit of around 10 minutes for this exercise.

Next, the group is to come up with as many other shared experiences as they possibly can. They would receive additional points for each of these. For example:

• Got a B on last report card
• Broke a bone this year
• Been stood up by a friend
• Went on a backpacking trip

Give the group five minutes to try to come up with as many of these common experiences as possible. Have the recorders list them on their sheets. Any experience is acceptable, as long as each person has shared that experience. At the end of the time limit, the group can total up its points.

This exercise really breaks the ice when youths see how much they have in common. *Syd Schnaars*

CROSS 'EM UP

On index cards, have each kid write one thing about himself that not everyone knows. Collect the cards

and use the information for clues to your own crossword puzzle, with the kids' first names as the answers in the puzzle. (See sample below.) Many computers have a crossword puzzle program that makes this project easier to complete. *Mark C. Christian*

COMMON KNOWLEDGE

This crowd breaker goes over big even if your group knows one another pretty well. Divide into small groups of five or six people each. Then have each person share one thing about himself that no one else in the group knows. ("My mother made me wear shorts to my first day of kindergarten because she thought I had cute legs.") After everyone in the group has shared, give a group assignment—find the most specific thing that they all have in common. Maybe everyone in the group had piano lessons or uses dental floss or went to Bible camp five summers in a row. Have each group share its findings with everyone else. *Marshall Shelley*

COMMUNITY QUIZ

This crowd breaker works best in situations when you know everyone who will be in attendance. You will need to contact each person in advance, get certain information from them, and then include that information in a written quiz that you use in a meeting or at an event. The quiz should contain

Cross 'Em Up

Across
1. Member of the drill team at Montgomery High
3. Father is a United Airlines pilot
7. Heavyweight wrestling champion
8. Family owns A & B Market
10. Friend of Anna's from Piner High School
11. Plays the drums in a band
12. Tennis star at Piner
15. Beatles fan
19. Loves any sport
21. On track team and student council
24. Enjoys classical music and guys
25. Our football hero
26. The Motorcycle Kid
28. The Hick
29. Just moved here from Texas
31. Has a last name like "Rock"
33. Esoteric (don't try to figure this one out, just write the word!)
34. Loves to dance
35. Loves horses

Down
1. Likes board games
2. Just got braces
4. Likes to play tackle football
5. Favorite sport is tennis
6. Loves to run track
7. Loves marine biology
9. Favorite hobbies: swimming, dancing, boys
13. Plays basketball
14. Grew up in Florida
16. Was in the play *Grease* at school
17. Recently injured left hand
18. Wants to be a stockbroker
20. Worked the light board at our school plays
22. Drives a '97 Mustang
23. Drives a '65 Mustang
27. Has a dog named Amos
29. Dad sells life insurance
30. Loves to golf
32. Collects stickers

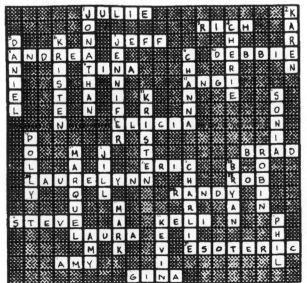

Common Ground

Category	Like	Dislike
Food		
Game		
TV Show		
Gift Received		
School Subject		
Chore at Home		
Song		
Hobby		
Way to Spend Saturday		
Sport		

Common Experiences

the same number of multiple choice or true-false questions as there are people (or you could have more than one question for each person).

You can then use the quiz in one of several ways. One way is to simply give everyone a copy of the quiz and have them mill around the room asking each other for the information needed to answer the questions correctly. At the end of a time limit, whoever has the most correct answers wins. Another way would be to have everyone take the test first, and then have each person stand up and give the correct answer as you go down the list of questions. The first suggestion is more active and requires more group interaction. A combination of both would be to have the kids take the test first and then mill around the room asking each person for the correct answers to see if they were right or wrong.

The key is to compose questions that are humorous and interesting and that include little-known facts about each person. It's not only fun, but very informative.

Some sample questions:
1. Danny Thompson is saving his money to buy—
   a. an airplane
   b. a hair transplant
   c. a moped
   d. a banjo
2. Lisa Burns likes—
   a. sardines
   b. artichokes
   c. cranberries
   d. Danny Thompson
3. Bill Florden's dad once appeared on "The Tonight Show."
   a. True
   b. False
4. Next Christmas, Paula Lovik's family is going—
   a. to stay home
   b. to Aspen, Colorado
   c. to her grandmother's house in Memphis
   d. to Japan

Tom Collins

COMPLIMENT CONTEST

If some of your kids have trouble saying nice things to each other, try this. It makes a competitive contest out of giving compliments.

Have the group sit in a circle and put one person in a chair in the middle of the circle. The person in the middle gets to choose two people: one will be complimented and the other will compete in complimenting with the person who is doing the choosing.

Both give their compliments, and the person who is the object of the compliments decides which compliment he or she likes the best. Of course, they may have trouble deciding, but they must choose one over the other. The person whose compliment was not chosen must then take the center chair.

A variation is to have the person in the middle be the recipient of compliments from two people he or she chooses. Then the winning compliment giver takes that person's place in the center and gets to receive compliments next. A game like this can help kids get used to the idea of building each other up.

Paul Mason

DROP THE BLANKIE

This is a great way to get everyone better acquainted. Before starting, make sure visitors are introduced, so that everyone has at least heard everyone else's name. Divide into two teams and have each team huddle at opposite ends of the room. Two people (neutral) hold a blanket in a vertical position, fully opened and touching the floor. Each team sends one person to stand one foot from their side of the blanket. When they are ready, the blanket is dropped. The first person to say the other person's name correctly captures that person for his team. The game continues until only one person remains on one of the teams. If neither of the last two players knows the other person's name, they are introduced and sent back to their teams. *Peter Torrey*

CONFUSION

This is a great crowd breaker for parties or socials. Type up the list below for everyone in the group; however, no two lists should be in the same order unless the group is very large. Each person is given a list and a piece of bubble gum. The winner is the first one to complete all ten things on their list in order. The idea is to have everyone doing something different at the same time. You won't be able to tell who is winning until the game is over. Anyone who will not do what someone asks him to do is disqualified.

• Get 10 different autographs: first, middle, and last names (on the back of this sheet).

• Unlace someone's shoe, lace it, and tie it again (not your own).

• Get a hair over six inches long from someone's head (let them remove it).

• Get a girl to do a somersault and sign her name here. _____

• Have a boy do five pushups for you and sign his name here. _____

• Play ring-around-a-rosy with someone and sing out loud.

• Do 25 jumping jacks and have someone count them off for you. Have that person sign here when you have done them. _____

• Say the Pledge of Allegiance to the flag as loudly as you can.

• Leapfrog over someone five times.

• You were given a piece of bubble gum at the beginning of the race. Chew it and blow ten bubbles. Find someone who will watch you do it and sign here when you have finished. _____

Marcie Stockin

FOOTBALL FRENZY

To break the ice at a fall meeting or during the Super Bowl season, hand out to each player a game sheet (see page 29) listing various activities. The object is to be the first person to complete (with a witness) each activity on the game sheet and get the signature of the witness beside the activity entry. Each of the 15 tasks must be signed by a different witness. *Steve Smoker*

FRACTURED FLICKERS

Contact the parents of the kids in your group and see how many short segments of home videos you can get of the kids when they were very young. Assure the parents that the videos will be returned. Splice a copy together and show it to the group at a party or social event. (Only a short segment is needed for each kid.) Have the kids try to guess people as they appear. Old home movies are great fun to watch, especially if you get some embarrassing shots of each kid in the group as a baby or toddler. *Joe Wright*

CRAZY SCHOOL DAZE MIXER

For this September get-acquainted game, give each student a copy of Crazy School Daze (page 30). The first player to have all assignments initialed wins. *Tom Lytle*

GUESS WHO?

For an easy get-acquainted activity, ask your kids to write down something about themselves that probably no one else knows. If they have trouble coming up with a unique contribution, suggest an unusual pet they might have or a weird snack or sandwich they like. If you get really desperate, ask for their mother's middle name. Collect all the responses.

As you read the clues aloud, have kids try to guess the identity of the cluegiver. Award 1000 points for each correct guess (have kids keep their own scores). For a prize, give away a copy of the church directory or an address book. *Jim Bourne*

HIDDEN NAME

This idea was used for a Valentine's Day event, but could be used anywhere. Each person is given a name tag and a sheet of paper containing valentine-themed sentences. In each name is hidden the name of someone present at the event.

• Please be generous with your love. (Gene)

• I'll be in a maelstrom if you won't be mine. (Mae)

• J'aime te, mon cher. (Jaime)

• Te adoro thy lips, love. (Dorothy)

As soon as a person deciphers the name out of the sentence, they are to get the signature of the person with that name. The names must be spelled correctly, but sometimes a word in a sentence may be misspelled to fit in the more difficult names: I've been in a nebeulahous state since I met you (Beulah). The one who gets the most signatures receives a prize. *Rowena Lee*

FOOTBALL FRENZY

RECRUITING YOUR TEAM

_____ 1. Recruit three people to join you in yelling one of the following: "We love the Dallas Cowboys" or "We hate the Dallas Cowboys." Request each person in your group to sign your game sheet.

SPRING TRAINING

_____ 2. Enlist someone to time you while you run in place for 20 seconds.

_____ 3. Recruit two people to perform four jumping jacks with you, counting out loud.

_____ 4. If you are a guy, find a girl with blue eyes and ask her, "Will you cheer for me today in the big game?" If you are a girl, find a guy with brown eyes and ask him, "Can I cheer for you in the big game today?"

THE BIG GAME

_____ 5. In a huddle with two other people, stack your hands on top of each other's and yell, "Go team!"

_____ 6. Persuade someone to gently tackle you.

_____ 7. Run up to someone you do not know well and say, "Put me in the game, Coach!" Be sure to get your "coach's" signature.

HALFTIME

_____ 8. You are in the band performing at halftime. Persuade someone to watch you pretend to play the trombone as you march from the back of the room to the front. Hum your school song as you march. Don't forget to ask your fan to sign your game sheet.

_____ 9. Lead another player in any cheer you know. If you can't think of a cheer, try this one: "Two, four, six, eight. Who do we appreciate?" Then yell the name of your youth pastor.

_____10. Run up to a person of the opposite sex and say, "Please put me in, Coach!"

_____11. Wad this paper into a ball. Ask someone to hike it to you and then run out to receive your pass. Throw the wad to the person. If either of you drops the wad of paper, you must repeat the activity. Then smooth out your paper for your receiver to sign.

_____12. Wow! You just scored the winning touchdown. Find a leader and give the leader a high five (slap a hand in the air) while yelling, "I scored the winning touchdown!"

BIG GAME WRAP-UP

_____13. Greet a friend and say, "I'm famous now! Can I give you my autograph?" Sign your friend's game sheet.

_____14. It's time to go to the locker room to change from your cleats to your shoes. Persuade another player to watch you take off your shoes and then put them on the wrong feet.

_____15. Report to the person conducting this game. If you are the first, second, or third person to complete the sheet, prepare yourself to win a prize!

Crazy School Daze

1. Find four people who don't go to your school, then form a train (hands on shoulders of the person in front of you) in grade order and cruise around the room reciting the Pledge of Allegiance. Have each member of your train initial here:

_____ _____ _____ _____

2. Remember the Rock-Paper-Scissors game? Find a partner to play Teacher-Principal-Parent. Stand back to back, count to three, then quickly turn around in the pose of a teacher (a "Thinker" pose—chin on fist), a principal (hands on hips, scowling), or a parent (shaking a finger in the partner's face). Teacher beats a parent, parent beats a principal, principal beats a teacher. The loser initials winner's sheet here:

_____

(Loser must play with different people until he or she wins.)

3. Find two other people. Lay on the floor, form the letter F and yell, "I should have studied more!" Have the other two people initial here:

_____ _____

4. Find someone of the opposite sex. Each of you add up the total number of letters in your first, middle, and last names. The person with the longest name gets his or her paper initialed here by the loser: _____ *(If you tie, you both win. If you lose, play with different people until you win.)*

5. Time for P.E.! Find three other people and play leapfrog. Everyone in your group must jump at least once. Have the two other frogs initial here:

_____ _____

6. Find someone for a match of Toe Fencing (face another player, clasp hands, and try to tap the top of your opponent's foot with your foot)—freshmen play juniors, sophomores play seniors. The first person to "strike" wins. If you win, the loser initials here:

_____

(If you lose, play twice more with different people; if you still lose, initial your own paper.)

I'VE GOT YOUR NUMBER

As kids arrive, each gets a number that they must wear in a conspicuous place on their clothes. Ahead of time, prepare lots of instructions on little slips of paper, then place them in a box. They should be things like:

• Borrow something from 1.
• Introduce 2 to 7.
• Have 6 get you a glass of water.
• Find out 12's middle name.

When everyone has their number, kids each take a slip of paper with an instruction on it. When they have completed the instruction, they come back and get a new one. At the end of the time limit (five minutes or so), whoever has completed the most instructions wins. Make sure you make plenty of instructions. *Arthur Crouse*

HUMAN CROSSWORD ✳

Make up a crossword puzzle similar to the sample below, with limbs that branch off at a variety of places in the puzzle. Plan your crossword so that several names of your young people will fit into the puzzle—but add some extra word-spaces that allow for kids' creativity. Award prizes to those who get the most names into their puzzle. *Glenn Embree*

I'D LIKE TO KNOW ✳

Want your group to know each other better? Give everyone a sheet of paper and a pen or pencil. Have kids write their names at the top of the sheets. Underneath their names they should write, "One

thing I really like about you is—" and, halfway down the sheet, "A question I've always wanted to ask you is—"

Now have them exchange papers, notice the name at the top of the sheet they have now, and finish each of the two sentences. Exchange several times so that each sheet has many affirmations of and questions about the sheet owner. When the sheets are returned to their owners, give the kids a few minutes to read what others wrote about them and to them. Then, one at a time, have your teenagers read and answer one question asked of them. Even if your group knows each other pretty well, there are bound to be some surprises. *Ed Laremore*

ICEBREAKER

Here's a mixer that takes the idea of an icebreaker literally. Kids sit in a circle (on the floor or around a table) with a bucket of square ice cubes close by. As players give their names, they place an ice cube on the ground or on the table on top of the previous cube. The goal is to stack the cubes as high as possible. If you want to keep the game going for awhile, start a new round of play whenever the stack of cubes topples. During each round, have kids reveal something different about themselves—their birthdays, favorite foods, favorite song or movie or TV show, etc. To add to the challenge, have players repeat the answers given by other players before allowing players to give their own answers. For example, if Judd is the fourth player in the favorite foods round, he must say "Kayly likes spam, Ethan likes macaroni and cheese, Keith likes pizza, and I like meatball sandwiches." *Keith Curran*

Human Crossword

Find, track, hunt down as many people as possible in the allotted time. Find out their first, middle, and last names and use one, two, or all three names in the puzzle. Letters must match up in adjoining names. Use the spaces below for those names that just don't fit. Nicknames are allowed (for example, Rodney/Rod: yes; Darren/Dar: no). Have fun and fill as many spaces as possible!

3 LETTERS

4 LETTERS

5 LETTERS

6 LETTERS

7 LETTERS

8 LETTERS

9 LETTERS

10 LETTERS

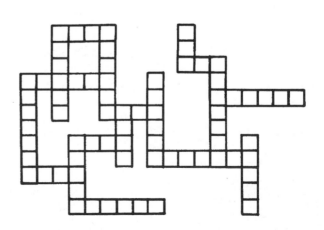

LICENSE-PLATE NAME TAGS

Give your kids blank license plates (paper or cardboard in the shape of a car's plates) and marking pens. Have them design creative, personalized license plates (like those you see on the road: KLU-LESS, N LUV, SWEET 16, etc.). Encourage a creative combination of numbers and letters. Limit

only the number of digits or letters that can be used on the plate.

Allow your teenagers to share the significance of their plates' messages and give prizes for the most original, humorous, creative, etc. They can be worn as name tags for the rest of the event. *Greg Fiebig*

IDENTITY

As your group enters the room, have them fill out a name tag and drop it in a basket. After all the teens have arrived, ask them to stand in a circle. Pass the basket around and have all the people take a name tag (not their name) without letting anyone else see the name.

Then ask everyone to turn to the left and place the name tag he is holding on the back of the person standing in front of him. The object of the game is to discover the name printed on the name tag pinned to his back. They find out their identity by asking yes-or-no questions like "Do I have red hair?"

or "Am I wearing jeans?" Each kid can only ask two questions of each person she meets.

When a person discovers whose name she has, she then goes to that person, places her hands on his shoulders and proceeds to follow him around the room. As more people discover their identities, the lines of people with hands on shoulders will lengthen until the last person finds his identity. *Craig Naylor*

INTERVIEW MIXER

Divide the group up into pairs. Give the group one or two minutes for each member of the pair to answer such questions as favorite subject in school, worst subject, favorite or worst moment, funniest moment, etc. Then call on certain members of the group to introduce their partner and answer the questions for them. Switch partners and use different questions. May be repeated effectively three to five times. *William C. Moore*

LET ME INTRODUCE MYSELF

Here's a crowd breaker idea for youths who know each other somewhat. Ask all the teens to write a short paragraph about themselves using the pronoun *I*. Tell them to be somewhat vague and to try to hide their identity, but to be truthful. Hand the paragraphs to a reader who will read them aloud and allow the others in the group to discuss the paragraph and then guess the writer's identity. Of course, the person who wrote the paragraph will have to remain elusive during the discussion. The object is to try and fool the group, which encourages kids to share things about themselves not already known. This works best with a group of about 10. *George E. Gaffga*

✳ ✓ LET'S GET ACQUAINTED

Photocopy the list on page 33 for each person in the group. Kids should fill in each blank with the signature of someone who fits the description. The first person to get all the blanks filled in or the one who has the most signatures at the end of the time limit is the winner.

Let's Get Acquainted

Directions: For each of the following items, get the signature of one student who fits the description.

1. I use Listerine: _____

2. My house has three bathrooms: _____

3. I've gotten more than two traffic tickets: _____

4. I have red hair: _____

5. I have been yelled at for spending too much time in the bathroom: _____

6. I have been inside the cockpit of an airplane: _____

7. I play the guitar: _____

8. I enjoy eating frog's legs: _____

9. I've been to Hawaii: _____

10. I use your brand of toothpaste: _____

11. I have used an outhouse: _____

12. I watch reruns of old sitcoms: _____

13. When I went water-skiing for the first time, I got up on my first try: _____

14. I know what charisma means: _____

15. I love broccoli: _____

16. I'm left-handed: _____

17. I carry a lighter or a book of matches: _____

18. I have a private bath at home: _____

19. I don't know your last name: _____

20. My last name sounds unusual: _____

ME GAME

e the party or meeting, look up in a name-your-
book the first names of all the students who
ttend. Write each name's original meaning on
l and distribute among your adult leaders
r keys that match meanings with names. Lay
e name cards on a table and, when the kids
......, ask them each to choose the card that they
believe reflects the meaning of their name.

Those who choose incorrectly must trade with
others until they all hold their names' correct meanings. Then, in pairs, students should answer at least
these questions for each other:
• How do you feel about the meaning of your name?
• Why were you given the name you have? (For
example, were you named after a relative or family
friend?)
• Where would you someday like to see your name?

(On a building, in a book, on a screen?)

After five minutes or so of sharing, regroup the
students and ask them to introduce each other with
the information they discovered. You may want to
give them this pattern to follow: "My friend here is
Jonathan; his name means gift of Jehovah, which he
thinks is cool. He was named for an uncle, and
someday he'd like to see his name in a book." *John
Berstecher*

MATCH MIXER

This is a great way to help kids in a youth group get
to know each other better. Give each person three
slips of paper or 3x5 cards. Have everyone write one
thing about themselves on each slip of paper.

Suggested items could be:
• The most embarrassing thing that ever happened
to me.
• My secret ambition.
• The person I admire most.
• My biggest hang-up.
• If I had a million dollars, I would . . .

All the cards are collected and redistributed
three to each person. No one should have one that
they wrote themselves. On a signal, everyone then
tries to match each card with a person in the room.
They circulate around the room and ask each other
questions to determine whose cards they have. The
first to do so is the winner. All the kids may be
allowed to finish and then share their findings with
the rest of the group. *Cecelia Bevan*

MATCH TAG

Give everyone a name tag with things written on it,
like favorite color, favorite musical group, favorite
movie of this year, favorite TV show, favorite place
in town to eat, etc. All the kids write in their own
answers and then put the tag on. After everyone has
filled out their tag, each person tries to find another
participant whose choices exactly match or are most
like theirs. *Joyce Crider*

NAME COUNT

This is a great game when you have lots of newcom-
ers in the youth group. Have the group form a circle
and choose someone to be in the middle. The person in the middle points to anyone, yells "right" or
"left," and then counts to five as quickly as possible
(must be understood, however). The person who has
been pointed to must yell out the person's name who
is on her right or left (whichever side was called)
before "It" counts to five; otherwise, she must be
"It." The group should get into a new circle, chang-
ing places, every so often. *Dan Sewell*

OH, NO!

Give everyone a few tokens, such as marbles, poker chips, clothespins, or whatever. Everyone should begin with the same number of tokens. Then allow the group to mingle and talk to each other.

Whenever someone says either "no" or "know," that person must give one of his tokens to the person with whom he is talking. It's difficult to avoid saying those two words in normal conversation, so this game produces lots of laughs. Give a prize to the one who collects the most tokens. *Charles V. Boucher*

MEET THE PRESS

First have the kids mingle and try to find out as much as possible about each other that they did not already know. After about five minutes have the group divide up into teams or smaller groups.

One person is then chosen at random to "Meet the Press." This person sits at the front of the room while each team receives some paper and a pencil. Each group must write the chosen person's name on the paper and a list of 20 truthful statements about him or her. Allow another five or 10 minutes for this.

When these are completed, they are then collected and read back to the entire group (one at a time). The team with the most correct statements is declared the winner. The person being described judges the statements as to their truthfulness.

In case of a tie, extra value can be given to statements that are less obvious. For example, "born in Nebraska" (unless you live there!) or "enjoys Shakespeare" shows more insight than "has red hair."

This exercise is not only fun, but promotes community within the group. You can adapt it in many ways, such as by having everyone make a list rather than in teams (best with smaller groups). You may also have more than one Meet the Press person per meeting. *Tom Bougher*

MY MOST EMBARRASSING BALLOON

Spread your group members out so they're two or three feet apart from each other. Blow up an extra-large balloon, and—while you pinch its neck—tell the kids that when you release the balloon and it finally comes to rest, whoever's nearest it must tell the group his or her most embarrassing moment.

Then let the balloon go. While the first victim is collecting their thoughts, a nearby student should blow up a new balloon in order to release it after the first player talks. This icebreaker works best when it continues rapid-fire, so keep it moving. *Todd Capen*

NAME SEARCH

The purpose of this activity is to get people who don't know each other to become familiar with the names of everyone in the group. Make sure there are no lists containing the names of the group visible anywhere; instead, put a large name tag on each person.

Give each person a word search puzzle with every person's name somewhere in the puzzle.

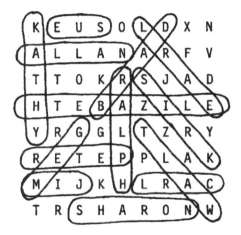

Of course, to do the puzzle, people have to know the names they are looking for, which means there will be a lot of walking around and looking at name tags. *Bruce H. Schlenke*

LABEL LAUGHS

Sheets of computer labels and marking pens are all you need for these two crowd breakers.

• **Tattoo.** This easy mixer doubles as a reminder that individual identities make a church body strong. Each player writes her own name on each label on the sheet. On a signal, kids begin to "tattoo" everyone else in the room with their labels. Players must introduce themselves to others before tattooing them.

The first person to run out of labels is the winner. A second winner is the one who collects the most labels. Before all the kids remove their tattoos, ask them to review the names they are stuck with.

• **Sticky Signatures.** In this variation, Allison (a fictitious player) must fill her sheet of labels with the signatures of others. After signing one of Allison's labels, the signer then detaches it from the sheet and sticks it on Allison's elbow, palm, nose—anywhere on her body that isn't already covered by a label (within the bounds of good taste, of course). Give a prize to the person whose body is covered with the most signatures within a time limit. *Pat McGlone and Becky R. Ker*

NAME-TAG MIXER

Here's a good suggestion for a mixer when people do not know each other very well. Make name tags that are about eight inches square for each person. In the middle write the person's name, but leave enough room on the name tag for other things to be written. When you are ready to begin, give each person someone else's name tag and have them find the person who belongs to it. After they have found that person, they can pin or hang the name tag on them. Once each person has his own name tag, he continues going around the room meeting people and asking each person he meets to autograph his name tag. After 10 or 15 minutes of this, stop and give a prize to whoever has the most names on their name tag.

PORTRAIT CONTEST

This idea is a lot of fun, and works well as a mixer if the students don't know each other very well. Give each person a couple sheets of art paper and some charcoal or felt-tip pens for drawing. Then have the kids pair off and draw each other's portraits from the shoulders up. Give them anywhere from 15 to 30 minutes to work. Have them write the subject's name on back of each one.

After the portraits are finished, number them and hang them on the wall. Hand out sheets of paper and pens and have the youths move around the room trying to guess which portrait belongs to whom. A prize can be awarded either to the one who drew the portrait with the most correct guesses

or to the one who guesses the most names right. You could also have them vote on the best portrait, the funniest portrait, and so on. *Kim Swenson*

NAME RIDDLES

This game requires an unusual dose of creativity on your part but can be well worth the extra effort. Make a list of the names of kids in your group and then try to make up a riddle or clue about each name. Most names can be used in some kind of riddle if you think about it long enough. Print the riddles on pieces of paper and let the kids mill about and try to fill in all the blanks, matching riddles with names. Below are some sample riddles to give you an idea of what can be done:

• What does a good mother do when her son comes to her, crying with a skinned knee? (Pat-terson)
• The tongue-tied sports announcer called the famous race between the rabbit and the _____! (Tuttle)
• Two things you do with coffee! (Brew-ster)
• What the man from Boston said he was going to do with his leaves. (Reich, pronounced Rike).
• When he talks about his fishing exploits, you know he is _____. (Lyon)
• What the hippie said when he was asked what was wrong with his lips. (Chap-man)
• A past-tense male. (Boyd)

Charles W. Stokes

✓ *Family Night*

POSITIVE PEOPLE BINGO

Try this crowd breaker at your next party. It works especially well with group members who are familiar with each other and who could use some affirmation—and who couldn't?

Find people who fit the descriptions on page 37. Then have them sign their first names in the squares that describe them. (Each person can sign your bingo sheet only once.) There will be two winners: one who has five signatures in a horizontal, vertical, or diagonal line; and one who has the most squares filled with signatures at the end of the time limit.

Nick Tomeo

POSITIVE PEOPLE BINGO

A GOOD FRIEND	SWEET	ENCOURAG-ING	A STRONG CHRISTIAN	KIND
HUMOROUS	HAS GOOD IDEAS	CARING	LOVING	GOOD
HELPFUL	IS EASY TO TALK TO	DARING	GENTLE	CRAZY (IN A GOOD WAY)
A LEADER	FUN	TALENTED	CONTENT	MAKES ME FEEL GOOD ABOUT MYSELF
A NICE SMILE	UNDER-STANDING	FRIENDLY	PATIENT	CREATIVE

MATCH-UP

Here's a good game that can be used as a crowd breaker or mixer. It really gets people talking and mixing with each other, and it's a lot of fun. Index cards are typed or written with statements like the one's listed below.

- I always eat bacon with my **eggs**.
- Tarzan lived in the jungle with his wife **Jane**.
- The worth of the American dollar is about **40 cents**.
- We could save on gasoline with fewer **"jackrabbit starts."**
- To get a mule's attention you must first hit him with a **board**.
- What good is a peanut butter sandwich without **peanut butter**?
- Speak softly and carry a big **stick**.

The words in bold are typed onto the small right-hand portion of the card, which is then cut off (see illustration).

The large and small portions of the cards are handed out at random to people with the instructions that they are to find the correct match with their portion. They must do this by going up to someone, introducing themselves, and then holding their cards together and reading them out loud. Some combinations can be very funny. If two people think they have a match, they must go to the designated leader, who has all the correct answers, and check to make sure. If they have a correct match, they can sit down. Another variation is to give everyone a large and small portion of cards which do not match and make them find both matches. *Kenneth Richards*

TWENTY TRIFLES

Pair kids up with those they don't know well; then distribute copies of the sheet on page 39. Tell kids to discover from each other the obscure facts asked for on the sheet. Players write down their partner's response. *Keith Curran*

STATISTICAL TREASURE HUNT

Divide the group into teams of equal number, if possible. Give each team a list of questions that are to be answered and evaluated as indicated on the sheet. Each team appoints a captain who acts as the gleaner of information and recorder. The game can be played around tables at banquet events.

Here is a sample of typical questions and methods of scoring. You can also use other questions that may be more appropriate for your particular group or occasion. *Angus Emerson*

SCRAMBLED NAME

Here's a great little mixer for larger groups (15 or more) that don't know each other. Pass out slips of paper and pencils and have everyone write down their own name with the letters all mixed up. In other words, if your name is Harvey Furd, then you might write it as "Vreahy Urfd."

When all the names have been put in a hat, have each person draw one out. On the command of "go," the kids try to unscramble the name on their paper either by themselves or with help from others. Once they know the name of the person, they must seek that person out—either by shouting out the person's name or by asking individuals their names. Once they find the person, they must have the person sign the piece of paper.

The game can continue until a time limit is up or until everyone has figured out all the names. *Bob Bilanski*

STICKER MIXER

Here's a good get-acquainted activity for larger groups. Write everyone's name on a sticker (round

TWENTY TRIFLES

_____ Favorite month of the year

_____ The worst radio station, in your opinion

_____ Your shoe size

_____ Grandparents' first names

_____ The longest time you ever went steady

_____ Have you ever driven a car?

_____ Do you like scavenger hunts?

_____ What you like most about Jesus

_____ What food you'd most likely order at McDonald's

_____ Your mother's maiden name

_____ Favorite place to sit in church

_____ Favorite biblical character

_____ Name of P.E. teacher

_____ Place of your birth

_____ Color of socks you're wearing

_____ Favorite flavor of ice cream

_____ Favorite drink

_____ Have you ever hit a home run?

_____ Do you like veggies?

_____ Show me, if you can, a scar. (Write down its location.)

ones work best) and distribute them at random. Have the teens stick the label on their face somewhere. Then everyone tries to find their own names on someone else's face. When a

teen finds her own name, she gets the sticker and sticks it on her shirt or coat and stays with the person on whom she found her name until that teen finds his own name. This is a good way for kids to see a lot of faces in a short time. *Don Rubendall*

WAKE-UP CALLS

Here's an idea that can be lots of fun, but it takes a little work. Get a group of youth sponsors together who are willing to get up early on Saturday mornings. Then go to several of your young people's homes before they wake up (with parents' permission, of course) and wake the kids in their bedrooms. Take a camera along and photograph them as they crawl out of bed, bleary-eyed in their pajamas. Then simply leave.

After collecting a good number of these pictures, use them for a hilarious slide show at one of your youth meetings. Kids will love to see each other looking half-asleep. This could be used as a fundraiser by asking kids to pay a certain amount to not have their picture shown. The money can then be donated to one of the group's mission projects. *David C. Wright*

TEN YEARS FROM NOW

This is a good way for kids to get to know each other better. Divide into groups of eight to 10. Have all the kids pick someone in their group they know the least and have them go off into some private

corner and ask each other questions such as:
• How has your personality changed (if any) in the last five years?
• What are some of the things that you really like to do?
• What are some of the things that you don't like to do?
• Do you have any hobbies? Name them if you do.
• Tell about an embarrassing situation from your past.
• Name something you are pretty good at.
• In what type of situation are you most comfortable? Uncomfortable?
• What are your favorite classes at school? Least favorite?
• What has been bugging you the most lately?
• Do you have any heroes—people you really admire?

Once everyone is finished, have them assemble into their groups and then ask all the kids to think about the person they interviewed and try to make a prediction about him, such as, "Ten years from now, he will be..." Have them share their predictions with the rest of the group. *Bob Gleason*

WHICH OF US AM I?

Copy the questionnaire on page 42 to pull out of kids little-known facts about themselves: favorite food, birth month and day, birth city, color of eyes, favorite vacation spot, favorite character in the Bible, favorite TV show, someone admired, favorite color, color of hair, favorite season of the year, one thing valued in life, hobby or interest (one that most of the group doesn't know about), favorite song, a world problem they consider significant.

As kids arrive, hand out the questionnaires for them to fill out—but without including their names. When all the sheets are completed, shuffle them and then tape them at random on the backs of the players. During this part of the icebreaker, players attempt to guess their new identities by asking other players yes-or-no questions about the information on their backs.

When players believe they know their "Guess Who?" identities, they remove the sheet from their backs, write their own names at the top and their new identities at the bottom, and turn them in. Number the sheets in the order they are received, since winners are the first three or four who correctly guess who they were. When all the sheets are collected, read through them one by one, allowing the entire group to guess whom the sheet is describing. Then ask the person it actually describes to stand. Award prizes to the three or four winners. *Tommy Baker*

WHOPPER

This is an interesting activity for groups that know each other fairly well. Instruct each person to tell the truth when giving two statements about himself, but to lie when giving a third. The whopper should sound reasonable and should not always be given last. Others try to guess which statement is the whopper. *Don Klompeen*

PEOPLE BINGO

Family Night

Give each player a bingo card of blank squares (see page 43). Players randomly fill the squares with the names of other players in the game. If there are left-over blanks, players can fill them in with an X. Fill a hat with the names of all the players written on small slips of paper. Randomly pull names from the hat and have kids mark an X through that name on their cards. The first person who has a row of Xs horizontally, vertically, or diagonally wins.

BIRTHDAY BARNYARD

This game works best with a large group. Give each person a list like the one below. Instruct players to look at the action described for the month of their birthday. When the lights are turned out, they are to stand up immediately and do the appropriate action. As soon as a player finds a person doing the same thing, the two lock arms and look for the rest of the team. As soon as all the team is together, they are to sit down. The first team to find all its members wins.

- **January**—shout "Happy New Year!"
- **February**—say "Be my valentine"
- **March**—puff up cheeks and blow (like a March wind)
- **April**—hop (like an Easter Bunny)
- **May**—say "Mother, may I?"
- **June**—say "Will you marry me?"
- **July**—make fireworks sounds
- **August**—sing "Take me out to the ball game…"

- **September**—fall down (like leaves)
- **October**—shout "Boo!"
- **November**—say "Gobble-gobble"
- **December**—say "Ho ho ho, Merrrry Christmas"

BEAN BLITZ

Each kid is given an envelope containing 20 beans. The kids then circulate around the room offering to someone else (one at a time) the opportunity to guess the beans in his closed hand. He approaches the person and says, "Odd or even." If the person guesses correctly, he gets the beans. If he guesses wrong, he must give up the same number of beans. A time limit is set, and whoever has the most beans at the end wins a prize. When a student's beans are all gone, she's out.

- **Seven Beans.** Everyone is given seven beans. The kids walk around the room asking each other questions. Every time they get the person they speak with to say either yes or no, they win a bean from that person. The game continues for 10 to 15 minutes. The person with the most beans wins a prize. *Jerry Summers*

Family Night

HUMAN BINGO

Give each person a Bingo card (like the sample on page 44). The squares are to be filled in with the signatures of people who fit the various descriptions. Each person must sign his or her own name. The first person to complete five blocks in a row gets Bingo. *Bobbie B. Yagel*

ACCIDENT REPORT

Equip players with a pencil and paper and instruct the group that on a given signal (such as two pie pans crashing together) they are to bump shoulders with someone close. After bumping, an accident report must be filled out getting each other's name, address, phone number, grade, driver's license number, etc. This can be continued six or eight times throughout the night's activities, each time bumping someone new. This is a good mixer and also a sneaky way of compiling a calling and mailing list for visitors. *Marv Walker*

Which of Us Am I?

Directions: If you're the one describing yourself by writing answers to these questions, do not sign your name. Sign your own name here when you've guessed your "Guess Who?" identity:

Birth month and day

Your city (address)

Color of eyes

Favorite vacation spot

Favorite character in the Bible

Favorite TV show

One person who has had a great influence on you (other than family member)

Favorite color

One thing you really value in life

Color of hair

Favorite season of the year

Hobby/interest (one that most don't know)

Favorite song

One thing you really value in life

A world problem that concerns you

Sign your "Guess Who?" identity here when you've guessed it:

PEOPLE BINGO

Human Bingo

Someone with two different colored eyes	Someone who owns a dog	Someone who is wearing contact lenses	A bilingual student (fluent in both languages)	Someone born outside the U.S.
Someone who owns a motorcycle	Someone who just ate at McDonald's	Sign your own name	Someone who likes to jog	Someone who can play a guitar
Someone with three brothers	Someone with blond hair at least 12 inches long	Someone who has been to Canada	Someone wearing blue socks	Someone who had a bad date last weekend
Someone who has a beard	An amateur photographer	Someone who weighs less than 100 pounds	Someone who drives a red car	Someone who has a cowboy hat
Someone with red hair	Someone who got an A in English	Someone who plays football	Someone who owns a horse	Someone who has broken a bone

MOTHER GOOSE PAIRS

As each guest arrives he or she is given a Mother Goose character or object and another youth is given a name taken from the same rhyme. The object is for the two characters from the same rhyme to locate each other without using questions or answers, but only sound effects and actions. For example, the boy falling off the stool and the marching soldier should soon get together as Humpty Dumpty and All the King's Men. *William C. Moore*

FAMILY CONFUSION GAME

Want to get parents and kids interacting and having fun? Distribute photocopies of the game sheet on page 46 and have extra pencils ready for those who need them. Then give the group a designated amount of time to complete the activities described. You may want to talk about the results afterward. *David C. Wright*

FOOD, GLORIOUS FOOD

Use the mixer on page 47 at your next banquet or food event. It could also be used as part of a Planned famine or other food/hunger awareness service project. *Daniel Harvey*

RATTLE TATTLE

Have your kids bring a dollar's worth of change with them to youth group, and start things off with this version of Bingo. Give each person a game sheet (page 48), then have the group mingle and find people who have coins as described on the sheet, or who can answer the questions correctly. Five in a row—up, down, or diagonally—wins. *Rick Jenkins*

COMIC STRIP MIXER

Take a Sunday paper comic strip (one that has about eight or nine frames to it), and cut it up into its individual frames. Take those frames and pin them on the backs of the kids in the group (one frame per person). When the game begins, the kids try to arrange themselves in the correct order, so that the comic strip makes sense. Since the frames are on their backs, it means that there will be a lot of communication required.

For larger groups, use several comic strips (preferably ones that have the same number of frames) and pin them randomly on everyone's back. The game now has the added element of finding others who have the same comic strip on their backs. The winning team is the first to line up with a completed comic strip in its correct order. *Lawrence E. Jung*

VOLLEYBALL DISCUSSION GROUPS

This game combines the fun of a volleyball game with some small group discussion. Divide into teams for a regular volleyball game. Then after every fifth (or so) point scored, have a row of players form a small group. The leader then throws out a discussion question like, "If you could go anywhere in the world, where would you go?" Each person gets a chance to speak, and then the leader gets the team going again. Since people are supposed to rotate after every volleyball point, the group will be different every time they get into small groups. It makes a great mixer. *Glen Bolger*

FAMILY CONFUSION!

1. The Woo-Woo Mixer

Find five others who were born in the same quarter of the year as you, identify yourself by making the appropriate sound as indicated below:

January/February/March: "Woo!"

April/May/June: "Woo-woo!"

July/August/September: "Woo-woo-woo!"

October/November/December: "Woo-woo-woo-woo!"

After all the folks in your group have found one another, hold hands, make a circle, and play ring-around-the-rosy. Then have one of your group members initial here:___

2. Family Vacation

Form a group with three other people so that it includes a dad, a mom, and two kids. Create a "train" at one end of the room, each person with his or her hands on the hips of the person in front, and with "Dad" at the head of the line. He leads the train across the room, zig-zagging back and forth from one end to the other. In the meantime, the kids should complain about how long it's taking, ask when they'll get there, and demand a stop for food or the bathroom. Then have your other vacationers initial here:___

3. Family Cooperation

Find any two other people. Sit on the floor back-to-back and with arms linked. In this position, the three of you must attempt to stand up together. After you've been successful, have a group member initial here:___

4. Sneak a Date (kids only)

Walk across the room with a member of the opposite sex without being spotted by your parents. If they spot you, you must try again later. Have your "date" initial here:___

5. Family Dinner Time

Form a group of five that includes both parents and kids (at least one of each). Sing together the commercial jingles for three or more fast-food restaurants. Have a group member initial here:___

6. Family Communication Practice

Find a kid if you're a parent, or a parent if you're a kid, and one extra person with a watch that times seconds. Cover your ears, face your "parent" or "child," and shout your favorite kid or parent lines for a full 10 seconds. Sample kid lines: "You never listen to me!" "All my friends get to do it!" "You don't trust me!" Sample parent lines: "When I was your age..." "I don't care who does it!" "As long as you're living under my roof..." Have the timekeeper initial here: ___

Food Glorious Food

1. Find two other people born in your same group of months by making the appropriate sound of your food group.
Jan/Feb/Mar —BREAD —"I've got the eaties for my Wheaties!" (sung)
Apr/May/June —MEAT —"Oink, oink, oink!"
July/Aug/Sept —VEGETABLES —Shout the name of your least favorite vegetable, e.g., "Beets, Beets, Beets!"
Oct/Nov/Dec —DAIRY —"Moo!"

2. Once you have formed your group of three, together name six edible objects that begin with the letter S. Have one of the group initial here:_____

3. Find a partner from somewhere in the room and together quickly shout, "Smorgasbords are disgusting!" seven times. Have your partner initial here:_____

4. Locate someone who likes liver (gag!) and have him or her initial here: _____

5. Grab a new partner and count each other's teeth. Write the number of teeth your partner has here:____.
Have him or her initial here:_____

6. Get another partner and see if you can "pinch an inch." If you can, tell that person he or she should eat more Special K. Have your partner initial here:_____

Rattle Tattle

A nickel minted between 1970 and 1975	<u>Exactly</u> 37¢ in change	A quarter more than 25 years old	17 pennies	Six coins all the same
A game token	A dime minted between 1981 and 1983	Whose picture is on the quarter?	Five dimes	A silver dollar
A penny made before 1950	A quarter with a small D on it	A foreign coin	Which president is on the dime?	No quarters
What does E Pluribus Unum mean?	What is the name of the building on the penny?	A nickel minted between 1951 and 1955	Exactly 63¢ in change	A 1972 quarter
A half dollar	Four quarters	A 1983 penny	A penny, a nickel, a dime, and a quarter	Someone who can flip heads three times in a row

MEETING–OPENING
CONTESTS

For these session starters you usually need two or three brave souls to participate in some crazy competition while the rest of the group watches. The result is a lot of laughter and applause. (All of these contests are good-natured and by no means demeaning; yet because there is some *potential* for embarrassment, go out of your way to affirm your courageous volunteers.)

FIND THE FACE

This activity works best when you have a large group in which everyone is not acquainted. Before the meeting, use an instant camera to shoot photos of three or four kids who are willing to make funny, distorted faces. Their goal should be to try to disguise themselves without using a disguise. Later, when everyone is together, give volunteers one picture each and have them comb the crowd for the person whose picture they're holding. The first person to identify and pull the right kid to the front wins.

BALLOON POP

Have several kids line up and give each one a balloon. The goal is to blow up the balloons until they pop. Increase the competition and include more people by creating teams and giving each team a small bag of uninflated balloons. The first team to blow up all its balloons until they pop wins.

APPLE-PEELING RACE

Several kids try to be the first player to remove the longest continuous strip of peel from an apple with a paring knife or a peeler. Give the winner a sack of apples, taffy apples, or a gallon of cider.

BACK BREAK

Have a youth come to the front and lie down across the seats of three chairs, supported at his head, rear end, and his feet. He then must remove the middle chair (under his rear end) and lift it over his stomach, then replace it under his rear end from the other side while remaining supported only by his head and feet. If any part of his body touches the floor, he loses and gets a penalty. Have three kids compete for the fastest time.

BOMBARDIER

Have pairs of kids come up to the front of the group. One person from each pair lies down on his back and holds a paper cup on his forehead. The other person must stand over her partner, break open an egg, and drop the contents into the cup. The pair who does the best job wins. *Bill Flanagan*

BOTTLE WALK

Here is a stunt that really takes strength. All you need is a couple of pop bottles (regular size), a starting line, and markers or chalk. The contestants—with feet behind a starting line and knees never touching the floor—grasp a bottle in each hand and "walk" on the bottles out as far as they can. Then they leave one bottle as far from the starting line as possible and "hop" back on the other bottle with both hands. The bottles must remain upright and the players must land on their feet, never having fallen. Carpeting is highly recommended. Height is a factor, but practice and technique count even more. The winner is the one who successfully places the bottle the farthest away. *Kathryn Lindskoog*

BROTHER AND SISTER

This game is reminiscent of the "Newlywed Game," but instead of newlyweds, you use brother-and-sister couples. They must work together to score the highest number of points possible to win. The brother is sent out of the room and the sister answers a series of questions about her brother. She records her answers on large sheets of paper. When the brother returns, he sits in a chair with the sister standing behind him holding up her written answers. Matching answers score points for the couple. Repeat the process sending the sister out of the room. Then tally the scores and award the prizes. You will find that their answers will produce some hilarious moments.

Sample questions to the sister about her brother:
• What is the craziest thing your brother has ever done?
• What is his favorite food?
• What do you like most about your brother?
• Describe your brother using only one word.
• What is the meanest thing he has ever done to you?
• What is his favorite color?
• What does he spend most of his time thinking

about?
• If you had one wish, what would you wish about your brother?
• What is his favorite TV show?

Sample questions to the brother about his sister:
• What does your sister spend most of her time doing?
• If you were your sister, what would you change about yourself first?
• About how many arguments do you have with her each week?
• Who obeys your mom and dad best, you or your sister?
• What animal is your sister most like?
• What is your sister's favorite subject?
• How often does she clean her room?
• How long does she usually talk on the phone?
• What did she do as a kid that got her in the most trouble?

You can vary this crowd breaker using other couples—friends, parent and child—by asking generic questions.

CANNED LAUGHTER

Fill a bunch of trash bags with empty soda cans and have three or more kids compete against each other

to see who can stack cans the highest within a given time limit. Give the winner a six-pack of soda.

CARROT DROP

Tie one end of a piece of string (about two feet long) around a carrot, so that the carrot will balance. Pin the other end of the string to the seat of a volunteer's pants. The object is to drop the carrot into a milk bottle (upright) without using the hands. It's really fun to watch.

CHOCOLATE DONUT FEED

Tie a donut onto several rubber bands so that the whole thing is about a yard long. Dip it into chocolate and while one kid is lying on her back, have another kid try to feed the donut to her. The donut usually bounces around like it's drunk, getting chocolate all over the person lying down. *John Splinter*

FRUSTRATION

Group A (two or more people) goes out of the room and selects a story, and then comes back in. Group B (two or more people) tries to guess what the story is by asking yes-or-no questions, such as "Is it about a boy and a girl?" "Does it happen in New Jersey?" However, what really takes place is the following: Group A goes out of the room and pretends to select a story, but what they really do is discuss the code they will use. For example, if someone from Group B asks a question in which the last letter of the sentence is a vowel, Group A will all answer yes. If it is a consonant, they will answer no. Group B in effect makes up their own story, without realizing it. The results are hilarious!!

For variation, if the last letter is a Y, Group A will answer, "Maybe." This usually frustrates Group B to the point where they will attack Group A! *Peter Poole*

CHECKER PUSH-UPS

Choose two players who think that they are the athletic type. They will compete to see who can stack three checker chips on the floor with their mouths while doing a push-up. Their bodies shouldn't touch the floor at all. Let them practice once before you time them one at a time. After a winner is declared, offer the loser another chance to win, only this time, blindfold both players. Time the loser while he does the push-up. After you blindfold the original winner so that he or she can try for another win, place a whipped cream pie on top of the chips; then stand back and enjoy the fun.

Here are some tips:
- Do not use shaving cream; the player will smell it.
- Use a different set of checkers for each player.

- Build this up as an athletic contest. Don't let it appear to be a trick or it may bomb.

CORN-SHUCKING RACE

Give each player an ear of corn that hasn't been shucked. Kids shuck the corn with their bare feet, no hands allowed. Whoever finishes first or whoever has done the best job within a given time limit is the winner. Award an appropriate prize such as microwave popcorn or a bag of corn chips.

CRAZY HAIRSTYLES

If your group is small, have everyone pair up for this game; otherwise you can select only three or four pairs from your large group. Let one person in each pair be the hairstylist, who must use shaving cream to create a hairstyle on his or her partner's head (one can of shaving cream per stylist). Have a panel of kids award prizes in different categories, such as weirdest hairstyle, most creative, ugliest, etc.

EGG DROP

If your group is small, have everyone pair up for this game; otherwise you can select only three or four pairs from your large group. One person stands over his or her partner, who is lying on the floor, face up. Give a plastic egg that has been weighted down with a marble to the person who is standing up. At the signal, that person is to drop the egg onto his or her partner's head. The players on the floor must lie with their hands flat on the floor alongside of them until after the eggs have been released. Only then can those players try to catch the egg before it hits. To increase the challenge, you might want to use real eggs instead of plastic ones.

FOOT WRESTLING

Try foot wrestling instead of arm wrestling. Have partners sit on the floor, lock toes, and at a given signal try to pin the other person's foot on the floor.

Egg Toss

Have partners line up facing each other, about three feet apart, and give each pair one egg. Partners are to toss the egg back and forth, each time taking one step backward. Whichever pair can keep their egg whole the longest wins. Alternate idea: Use water balloons instead of eggs.

Face Decorating

Have several partners participate in this one. One person is given items necessary for cake decorating (squeeze tubes of icing, whipped cream, candy sprinkles, etc.) and they decorate their partner's face. The decoratees should lie down to be decorated, then stand to have their faces judged, either by the audience or a panel of judges. *Ben Smith*

Swinging Marshmallow

Pair up the kids (player A and player B) and give each pair a four-foot-long piece of string and two marshmallows. At a signal the pairs tie one marshmallow on each end of the string. Player A in each pair holds one marshmallow in her mouth while

standing and facing the front of the room. Player B stands to the side of player A at an arm's length, looking toward player A. Moving only her head, player A begins to swing the string back and forth like a pendulum while player B attempts to catch the swinging marshmallow in his mouth. Player B may move only his head. The winner is the first pair in which player B catches the marshmallow. *Greg Miller*

Foot Painting

Figure out how many letters are in the name of your group or church and select half as many volunteers as there are letters. If you have an odd number of letters, round high. (For example, if you have 17 letters, select nine volunteers.) Tell the volunteers to sit on the floor facing the audience and to take off their shoes. Paint one letter on the bottom of each foot, scrambling the letters as you go. Use a felt marker or poster paint, and write big. At a signal, they try to unscramble the letters and make the name readable without getting up or moving from their positions.

Whistle and Burp

Give five saltine crackers to each of five players and a can of soda to each player's partner. At the signal, the players eat their crackers and whistle while their partners drink the whole can of soda and burp. The first pair to finish wins. Both partners on the team must succeed at their responsibility to win.

Forty-Inch Dash

Cut 40-inch pieces of string and tie a marshmallow to one end of each piece. On a signal, each person puts the loose end of the string in his or her mouth and, without using hands, eats his or her way to the marshmallow. The first person to swallow the marshmallow is the winner. For prizes, you could award ingredients for making s'mores—graham crackers, chocolate bars, and marshmallows.

Glove-Milking Contest

Partially fill two large rubber gloves with milk. Hang each glove from sticks. Have two helpers quickly punch the same number of pinholes in the ends of the fingers at the same time on both gloves; then let two contestants try to milk the gloves over two buckets. Whoever gets the most milk into his or her bucket within the time limit wins.

Grape Grab

Make flavored gelatin ahead of time—enough to fill a couple of aluminum pie pans. Before refrigerating them, drop five whole grapes into each pan. Have three contestants try to retrieve the grapes from the gelatin and place them in plastic cups using only their teeth, not their hands. The winner is the first person to get all five grapes in the cup or to get the most grapes in the cup within a time limit.

GREASEPUFF

This game is not only fun, it is funny. Give each contestant two plates (preferably tin, paper, or plastic). Have them place the two plates in front of them, side by side. Contestants count out 25 cotton balls, put them in the right plate, and then put an adequate supply of Vaseline on their nose. With hands behind their backs, the object is to see who can be the first one to move all their cotton balls from the right-hand plate to the left-hand plate without the use of hands or tongue. They can blow or twitch with their noses. Winner receives all the cotton balls and a jar of partially used Vaseline. *Anna Dail*

HANDCUFF HASSLE

Have a couple face each other. Both people are handcuffed with the ends of a three-foot string tied to their hands. However, one partner's string is behind the other's so that they are linked together. The object is to get free without untying the strings or breaking the strings. Secret: To escape, pass the center of one partner's string through the wrist loop and over the hand of the other partner.

HANG IT ON YOUR BEAK!

With only a package of plastic teaspoons and a little practice, you'll break up your crowd in no time! First (at home), practice hanging a spoon on your nose. You'll have to rub the oil off your nose with your shirt sleeve, and then breathe heavily on the inside of the spoon. Then hang it on the end of your nose!

After you teach your crowd this, uh, trick, then start some competition:
• See who can hang a spoon off their schnozz the longest.
• See who can get the spoon off the ends of their noses and into their mouths—using only their tongues.
• See who can hang a spoon off any part of their faces or arms.

Award comic prizes to the winners. And bring along some spoons of varying sizes and style and let the kids try them on for size! *Carley Toews*

HOUDINI

Have three pairs (boy and girl) come to the front of the room and interview them. Then give each girl a 20-foot length of rope. The girls have three minutes to tie up the boys as tightly as possible. After they are tied up, the guys race to see who can get completely out of the rope in the fastest time. The guy who gets untied the quickest wins a prize for his pair. Encourage the girls to tie up the guys as tightly as they possibly can, by having the guys, perhaps, lie down on their stomachs and then tying their hands and feet together, etc.

LEMON-EATING RACE

Give a lemon to each of three daring volunteers. At the signal, their goal is to be the first to peel a lemon and eat all of it except for the seeds and peel.

LEMONADE-EATING CONTEST

Instead of drinking homemade lemonade, three contestants eat the ingredients separately, figuring that the items will mix together in their stomachs. They should each drink a large glass of water, eat a raw lemon (not the peels or seeds), and then eat a tablespoon of sugar. First person to finish wins.

LICORICE EAT

Give everyone in the group a piece of licorice (the kind that comes in strips about a foot long). Have them put it about one inch into their mouths and, at a signal, eat the rest of it without using their hands. It's surprising how difficult this can be for some kids. The last person to finish eating receives a penalty. *Len Kageler*

LONG JOHN STUFF

Find two pairs of extra-large long underwear and have two kids put them over their clothes. Have the rest of the group blow up a bunch of balloons (50 large balloons or 100 small ones). Then have two assistants, who are the same sex as the contestants, help to stuff balloons into their partner's long johns at every accessible point. The goal is to be the one with the most balloons in your long johns at the end of a two-minute time limit. Count the balloons while they are still in the long johns by carefully popping them with a pin.

LOOPING THE LOOP

Give each person a strip of paper about 1½ inches wide and a foot or so long. Also, provide scissors and Scotch tape. Have them make the strip into a loop and twist it once, joining the two ends carefully with the tape. (If you use gift-wrap paper, the colored side of the strip meets the white side at the junction where they are taped.)

You have now created a Möbius strip, a one-sided geometrical figure discovered in the 1800s by a famous German mathematician named Möbius. Draw a line down the center of the strip continuously, and you will mark the entire strip on both sides without ever lifting your pencil. You end up where you began. This proves that the figure has only one side.

Next, if you use a pair of scissors to cut along your center dividing line all the way around, the loop becomes suddenly twice as big, but it is no longer a Möbius strip. It has two sides again. Finally, cut this longer, thinner loop of paper right down the middle all the way around. What do you get? Not a longer loop this time but two linked loops.

What all this proves has not yet been determined, but with a little creativity it can undoubtedly be applied to something. *Kathryn Lindskoog*

MARSHMALLOW DROP

Have six kids pair up. Three of the kids lie down on the floor while their partners drop large marshmallows dipped in chocolate syrup into their mouths from a height of about four feet. The players must catch the marshmallows in their mouths and eat them. Whoever eats the most marshmallows within a time limit that you set is the winner. Deduct points for marshmallows that fall on the floor.

MONSTER MAKEUP

Spread out lots of plastic on the floor and have plenty of towels on hand. Select three pairs of kids for this event. Have three of the volunteers sit in chairs facing the group. Have their partners give them a free makeup session using cosmetics such as peanut butter, toothpaste, jelly, bread crumbs, and other messy items. The audience judges who ends up with the ugliest makeup treatment.

THREE-LEGGED JEANS

Prior to the meeting, sew several pairs of old blue jeans together in the following manner: Rip out the outside seam of one leg on two pairs of jeans and

sew the two pairs together (see diagram abbove). Use baggy jeans. Pairs must get into the jeans and at a signal, race to the goal. *Larry Houseman*

MUMMY

Have six kids break up into groups of three. Give each group plenty of rolls of toilet paper or paper towels. One player on each team is to be wrapped head to toe like a mummy by his or her teammates. Award a prize for the best-looking mummy.

MUSICAL HATS

Have six teens stand in a circle, facing in the same direction. Five of the six players put hats or large plastic bowls on their heads. At the signal or when the music starts, each player continuously grabs the hat from the head of the person in front and puts it on their own head until the music stops. Then whoever is left without a hat at that point is out of the game. Make sure there is always one less hat than there are players. When there are only two players left, they stand back to back, grabbing the hat from each other's head. The last one to have a hat on when the music ends is the winner.

NOODLE WHOMP

Have two players get down on all fours, facing each other and wearing blindfolds. They join left hands. Each player has a rolled-up newspaper and gets three tries to hit the other player with it. The person being swung at can move anywhere to try to get out of the way but cannot let go of the other player's hand. Whoever gets hit the most times is the loser. Try it with different pairs.

NOSE ART

Tape three large sheets of paper (two or three layers deep) on the wall or set up three easels at the front of the room with drawing paper attached. Select three volunteers to paint on the drawing paper with poster paint applied with their noses. Vote on the best painting.

NOSE BALANCE

Have a couple of kids sit on chairs facing the audience. Tell them to lean their heads back so that you can balance a penny on their nose. Their goal is to wiggle the penny off their noses without moving their heads. The first person to knock the penny off wins.

PANTYHOSE RACE

Get two pairs of queen-size pantyhose. Have two players take off their shoes and put on one pair of pantyhose over their socks and clothes while wearing gardening gloves. The winner is the first person to pull the pantyhose over the hips.

NOSE WASHING

Have three pairs come to the front of the room. Place a glob of shaving cream on the nose of one person from each pair. From six feet away their partners race to clean the cream off by using squirt guns.

OBSTACLE COURSE

Create an obstacle course using tables, chairs, and anything else that is nearby. Then send a few volunteers out of the room and blindfold them. Bring them back to the obstacle course one by one after you have removed all of the obstacles. Let them carefully work their way around the nonexistent obstacles. Then surprise them when you remove their blindfolds.

PIE-EATING CONTEST

It's old, but it's still one of the best fun things around. Have a race in which teens devour cream pies with no hands. Put a time limit on it and give prizes for the most cream pie eaten, the messiest face, the neatest eater, etc.

PING-PONG BALL RACE

Give each player a Ping-Pong ball and a party horn that uncoils when you blow into it. Players push the balls across the floor using only the horns. They cannot blow air directly on the ball or touch it in any way. The winner is the first player to cross the finish line.

SODA BOTTLE PICKUP

See who can stand on one foot, hold up the other foot with one hand, and try to pick up a standing soda bottle with his or her teeth. Whoever can do it in the shortest time wins. Whoever falls over is out.

POPCORN STUFF

Ask for a couple of volunteers who think they can hold more grapes, marshmallows, or popped corn in their mouths than anyone else. Have other kids count each piece the players put in their mouths. No swallowing is allowed.

PUT YOUR MONEY WHERE YOUR MOUTH IS

Two kids who have wallets face each other to see who can "draw" his wallet the fastest and stick it in his mouth, gunfighter style. Another way to do this is to ask for two kids who want to win two dollars. When they come up, give each a dollar bill, which they must put in their wallets, and place back in their hip pockets. On your signal, they must go for their wallets, gunfighter style, and each must take the dollar out of his wallet, put it on the floor, and then sit on it. Last teen to do so has to give the other guy his dollar, and he loses. *Joe Rice*

QUICK-DRAW CONTEST

Have two people stand back-to-back with one of them facing the group and one of them facing an easel or chalkboard and holding a marker or chalk. Give the person facing the group a small item such as a lightbulb, screwdriver, or remote control. He or she describes it to the partner who draws it without looking at the object. Players can't describe how the object is used. Time one pair of players at a time; then declare a winner with the best time. To make this game easier for younger players, allow the person who is describing the object to watch the artist at work.

RUBBER BAND RELAY

Put a rubber band around each player's head. Make sure that it crosses over the tip of the nose. Players are to use their facial muscles to work the rubber bands down to their necks without using their hands.

SHOE STRETCH

Remove the shoestrings from two old pairs of men's shoes, size large. Punch a hole in the back of the shoes and tie a four-foot piece of elastic (sold in fabric stores) to each shoe. Place two chairs about 20 feet apart and tie the other ends of the elastic to the legs of the chairs (one pair of shoes per chair). Then have two teens put on the shoes (untied), walk toward each other, and exchange shoes—all without using their hands. If any shoe snaps back to the chair, the players must start over. Have several two-person teams compete to see who can do it in the least amount of time. Have people sit on the chairs to weigh them down.

SHOE TIE

Get the word out in advance that everyone should try to wear shoes that lace up. Have people pair up. One person in each pair must untie one of his or her shoelaces. The other person must try to tie the shoelace while using only one hand and anything else but the other hand. The winners are the first pair to finish.

SHOULDER PIN

Have two kids sit back-to-back on the floor, lock arms, and try to pin the other person's right shoulder to the floor. It's sort of like arm wrestling, except that you use your whole body.

SNOOT SHOOT

The idea of this game is to see how far players can propel a Kix, Cheerio, or other bit of breakfast cereal across the room—using the air from their noses! To play, mark out a line behind which each player must stand. They must then place the Kix in one nostril

of their choice. When you say "Fire!" they should hold the other nostril shut and exhale through their noses with as much force as possible. Furthest distance wins.

This is a great icebreaker, or it works well as one event in a series of relays or target-shooting contests, with each team choosing a representative to compete. *John K. Larson, Jr.*

SOAP SCULPTURE

Give each pair of players a can of shaving cream. They should shoot a large glob of cream onto a table covered with plastic or onto a plate. Give them two minutes to sculpt it into anything they want. The audience judges the best job.

SPAGHETTI ON TOP

Give several pairs of volunteers a bowl of cold, cooked spaghetti. Have one person in each pair arrange a spaghetti hairstyle on his or her partner's head within one minute. Present awards in various categories such as most natural hairstyle, weirdest, etc.

SQUIRM RACE

Place a volleyball (or ball of similar size) between the foreheads of a pair. Without using their hands, they must work the ball down to their knees and back up again. Their hands must be kept behind their backs, and the two must start over if they drop the ball. *Bryan Pearce, Jr.*

STANDING BROAD GRIN

Measure everyone's grin with a ruler to see who has the widest smile. Offer first, second, and third place prizes to the biggest mouths. (Prizes are toothpaste, mouthwash, toothbrushes, sugarless gum, dental floss, etc.)

STRAW MUMBLE

Have three guys come to the front of the room. Each gets a plastic drinking straw. The idea is to get the entire straw inside your mouth by chewing. No hands allowed. It is harder than you think. First person to do so wins. *Roger Copeland*

TIPTOE THROUGH THE INDEX CARD

Give each participant a 3x5 card and a pair of scissors. Explain that this is a contest to see who can cut a hole and "step through the card" first. It can be done.

This can be done by properly cutting the card:
1. Fold the card in half and cut along the lines as shown in Figure A below.
2. Then open the card and cut along the fold, being careful not to cut the card in half, as shown in Figure B.

When the card is opened up, a loop large enough to step through is formed. *William Chaney*

Tiptoe through the Index Card

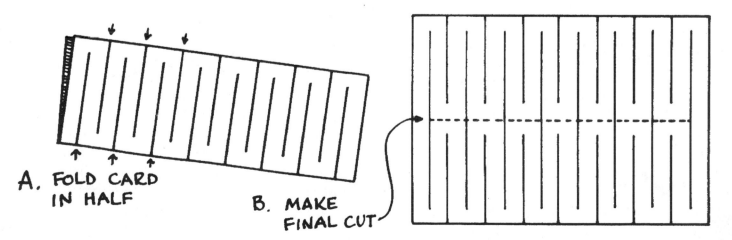

A. FOLD CARD IN HALF

B. MAKE FINAL CUT

STRAWLESS RELAY

Have three or four kids put one end of an ordinary drinking straw in each of their mouths. Have them all start at the same time and try to get their mouth from one end of the straw to the other without using hands. The only legal way to do this is by using their mouth and tongue. The facial expressions will have the audience in stitches. *Brad Winkler*

TEN TOES ON THE ROCKS

Fill two pans with crushed ice and place 10 marbles in the bottom of the pans, underneath the ice. Two players must remove their shoes and socks and try to

get the marbles out of the pan using only their toes. They cannot turn the pan over or spill any ice. The first player to get all the marbles out of the pan is the winner.

SQUEEZE PLAY

Two people face each other. Place a large balloon between them. Time the pair to see how fast they can break the balloon by body pressure alone. The fastest pair wins.

SPEECH SPASM

A teen tries to earn a five-dollar bill by saying two simple words: *toy* and *boat*. First the teen says the words slowly. Explain that it is just to make sure that he or she can pronounce them at all. (Have the audience applaud.) Then he must say the two words together (10 times in five seconds) in order to win the money. The words must be pronounced correctly.

It is unlikely that anyone will win the money.

TOMATO TEST

Three pairs of kids place a tomato between their foreheads. While holding it there without using their hands, one player tries to put a shoe on her partner's foot.

WHIRLING HIGH JUMP

Get three volunteers to come forward and try this simple game. Give each a stick about 18 inches long. Tell them to hold it straight out at arm's length with both hands so that they can watch it while turning around fifty times. They then must drop the stick and jump over it. Whoever jumps the farthest is the winner. Most kids get so dizzy they can't even see the stick when they drop it, let alone jump over it. It's fun to watch. Have the rest of the group count as the person turns around. *Kent Johnson*

TONGUE-TIE

Have three young people come up to the front. Each is given a piece of wrapped bubble gum. On a signal, the players put the gum in their mouths, wrapper and all, and must unwrap the gum in their mouth (no hands), spit the wrapper out, chew the gum, and then blow a bubble. First one to do so wins a prize. *Joe Rice*

WATER BALLOON SHAVE

Three players sit in chairs facing the audience and each holds a large water balloon on her head. Their partners cover the balloons with shaving cream and, with a single-edged razor blade (no razor, just the blade), try to shave all the soap off of the balloon without breaking it. Whoever is the first to succeed is the winner.

TOOTHPASTE CATCH

Three volunteers lay on the floor, face up, with a small paper cup in each of their mouths. Their partners stand above them and try to fill the cup with toothpaste by squeezing it out of the tube and letting it drop from at least three feet high. Give toothbrushes to the winners.

UN-BANANA

See who can be the first to peel a banana, eat it, and drink a can of soda. Give the winner a bunch of bananas and a six-pack of soda.

MUSICAL
CROWD BREAKERS

CROWD BREAKERS

...faloes with strep ...peners. The best ...them require lit- ...g warblers.

ROW, ROW, ROW YOUR—

...but it's a lot of fun. Instead of ..., Row Your Boat" in a round, try ...after each time you sing the song

...our boat, ...e stream, ..., merrily, merrily, ...am.

...our boat, ...e stream,

Merrily, merrily, merrily, merrily,
Life is but a...

3. Row, row, row your boat,
   Gently down the stream,
   Merrily, merrily, merrily, merrily,
   Life is but...

...and so on until no more words are left. *Sarah Poythress*

• Second time, have them cough every time the word *cold* comes. Don't sing *cold*.
• Third time, have them thump their chest when the word *chest* comes. Don't sing *chest*.
• Fourth time, have them rub hands together every time the word *rubbed* comes. Don't sing *rubbed*.
• Fifth time, have them hold their nose when the words *camphorated oil* come. Sing *camphorated oil*.
• Each time you keep adding the motions. At the end speed up. Makes for a wild coordination test.

Jim Green

SING SONG SORTING

This game is great as a way to divide a crowd into

teams or small groups. Prepare ahead of time on small slips of paper an equal number of four (or however many groups you want) different song titles. As people enter the room, they receive (at random) one of these song titles. In other words, if you had 100 kids and you wanted four teams, there would be twenty five each of the four different songs. On a signal, the lights go out (if you do this at night) and each kid starts singing the song he received as loudly as possible. No talking or yelling, only singing. Each person tries to locate others singing the same song. The first team to get together is the winner. Song titles should be well-known. *Arthur R. Homer*

EARPHONE SING-ALONG

Nearly all of us have at one time or another embarrassed ourselves by singing loudly (and often off-key) while listening to a Walkman. So make a contest of it!

Announce that a prize (perhaps an inexpensive Walkman) will be given to the student who does the best job of performing a favorite song to taped accompaniment. (They must have tapes of their songs.) If your students are natural hams, you may

want to wait until the performance to tell them that they will hear the tape through earphones. You might want to say something like this: "Oh, by the way—you'll hear your tape on a Walkman, and the audience will hear only your voice. And the more creative the choreography, the higher your score." Ensure that the volume is high enough in the earphones so that the contestants cannot hear their own voices clearly.

The performances are inevitably so off-key that the audience will need time to stop laughing between contestants. Give participation prizes to everyone and the Walkman to whomever you or the judges deem to be the most entertaining. *Randy Phillips*

STORY SONG SKITS

Remember the songs we listened to as children? Over and over we played them, until we knew every word. Here is a way to use all of those old familiar story-songs and get a good laugh with your group.

Divide your group into several smaller groups and give each group a cassette/CD recording of one of these children's songs. (Check local music stores in the children's sections for songs if necessary. The cornier, the better!) Each group should also get a cassette player/CD player.

Each group must pantomime the entire song—music, speaking parts, narration, movements—and dress accordingly. Give them enough time to prepare their outfits and practice a little. Then take turns presenting the story-songs. The result is great! And to ensure plenty of long-lasting laughs, videotape it! *Doug Newhouse*

TOP 40

This fun guessing game is a quick crowd breaker. Tape record bits and pieces of some of the Top 40 hits of the month, week, or year onto a cassette. You can usually accomplish this by recording them right off the radio. Edit it so that only a second or two of each song can be heard. Then when you play it back for the teens, see how many of them can identify all of the songs. Usually kids are so familiar with these songs that it is nearly impossible to stump anyone, even when you play only one second of each song. This would be a good opener for a meeting that includes a discussion on popular music or a similar topic. *Richard Mallyon*

UP AND DOWN BONNIE

Here's a great variation of the song, "My Bonnie Lies over the Ocean." While singing the song, have everyone stand on the first word that begins with a **B** and sit down on the next word that begins with **B**. Continue the same process on all the **B** words. For variation, have half the group start the song standing up. People get confused about whether they are to be standing or sitting. It's lots of fun. *Darrell Simpkins*

THE TWELVE DAYS OF CLASS

Using the tune to "The Twelve Days of Christmas," here's a song to sing just after Christmas vacation, during finals week, or any time your kids feel overwhelmed by school:

On the _____ day of school, my teacher gave to me: _____

(Insert the words below in the blanks for the 12 verses.)

First day: A headache when the final bell rang
Second day: Two study halls
Third day: Three pop quizzes
Fourth day: Four research projects
Fifth day: Five themes to write
Sixth day: Six math problems
Seventh day: Seven book reports
Eighth day: Eight Home Ec projects
Ninth day: Nine lab experiments
Tenth day: Ten biology dissections
Eleventh day: Eleven art assignments
Twelfth day: Twelve history books to read

Another way to enjoy this song is to write the verses on pieces of paper and have each person draw one out of a hat or bowl. Give kids five minutes to find others with that same verse. Then sing the song together on the first line, with each group singing its assigned part as it comes up in the song. *Allen Johnson*

THE TWELVE DAYS OF SCHOOL

Here's a fun song that the group can sing, or you can do it as a skit with one person taking each line and acting out each part. It should be sung to the tune of the "Twelve Days of Christmas."

"On the first day of school, my mommy said to me..."

First day: "Don't ever wet your pants."
Second day: "Don't lift your dress."
Third day: "Don't eat your crayons."
Fourth day: "Don't chew gum."
Fifth day: "Don't pick your nose."
Sixth day: "Don't hold hands."
Seventh day: "Don't throw spitballs."
Eighth day: "Don't ever belch."
Ninth day: "Don't sleep in class."
Tenth day: "Don't be a sissy."
Eleventh day: "Don't bite your toenails."
Twelfth day: "Don't kiss the girls (guys)."

STUMP THE BAND

When Johnny Carson hosted "The Tonight Show," he regularly played this game. Your version of it might be to have the staff or sponsors of your youth group at the front of the room, while the leader goes into the audience to pick out volunteers, who try to name a song that the staff doesn't know. The song has to be legitimate; no on-the-spot composing. If the staff can sing it, they get the praise and admiration of the audience. (Applause) If they don't know it, the volunteer must sing their song in order to win a prize. Possible prizes are:

• A free chicken dinner (give them a live chicken).
• A sleeping bag (a "bed" with a paper bag "sleeping" in it).
• Half a haircut.
• A certificate for a free sewer inspection.
• A candlelight dinner for two (at the city rescue mission).
• Answer sheets to 1933 math test.

Think of your own crazy prizes.

QUIZZES AND
WORD GAMES

After a week of pressure-packed pop quizzes, reviews, and exams at school, your kids may be relieved to take a quiz or play a word game that has absolutely no academic consequences. Here are logic problems, word searches, and more—with a few laughs thrown in for good measure.

COMPUTER SPELLCHECK

When spellcheck tags a misspelled computer document, it probably suggests alternative spellings to replace the original word you used.

So have some fun: spellchecking proper names produces some hilarious substitutions (which are, on occasion, strangely accurate). The name Duffy Robbins, for instance, brings up Puffy Robbing. Tony Campolo becomes Tony Carpool. The contributor of this idea becomes Ralph Realigned, Reloaned, or Reliant.

Ask the computer buffs in your group to run the youth directory through spellcheck, then choose the funniest alternative names and write them on name tags to use at the next youth activity. Kids who arrive must first of all find their own name tags; then they all can vote for the most outrageous name, the most accurate description generated by the computer, etc. Students with winning names receive awards.

Ralph Rowland

NAME THE NEIGHBORS

A fun problem of logic—that might come in handy sometime when you want to keep a group occupied—is on page 72. Here's the solution (from west to east on the street):

Angus Emerson

CRAZY BIBLE CLUES

Here's a word game that involves names and books of the Bible. Each kid is given the list of clues (see page 74) and asked to write in the biblical name that fits each clue. While it's only a game, it can help kids remember names and places in the Bible.

Thinking up clues like these can be just as much fun as solving them. Have the kids divide into teams and allow each group to come up with 10 of its own

Name the Neighbors

Fran, Grace, Helen, Ida, and Jane and their husbands all live on a certain street that runs east to west in the town of Centerville. From the following clues, give each couple's full names and describe exactly where on the street each couple lives.

- Grace has Ralph as one next-door neighbor and the Greens as her other next-door neighbor.

- The Browns live in the westernmost house—Ned in the easternmost.

- Sam has Ida as one next-door neighbor and Peter as his next-door neighbor on the other side.

- Both Jane and Peter live east of the Whites.

- Peter lives next door to the Blacks.

- Tom lives west of the Greys and east of Grace.

- Helen and Jane are next-door neighbors. The Greys live next to Jane also, but on the other side.

clues. Here's how to do it:

First, think of the word or name you will be using as the answer. Second, imagine what that word or name immediately brings to your mind by association, sound, or spelling. Then, write a sentence that describes it and—presto!—you have a crazy clue. Like this:

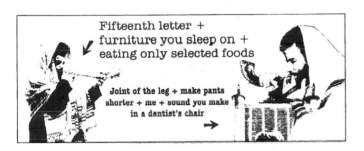

Fifteenth letter +
furniture you sleep on +
eating only selected foods

Joint of the leg + make pants
shorter + me + sound you make
in a dentist's chair →

Collect the clues from all the teams. If you have time, make a master list of clues, make copies, and distribute them for everyone to solve. Otherwise, read clues aloud one at a time and have each team record its answer privately. Then go through the answers together and score like this: Each team gets one point for solving a clue from any other team and one point for every clue it has written that stumps the rest of the group. If the total group (by consensus) agrees that the unsolvable clue is misleading or poorly written, however, then no points are awarded.

Here are the answers:
1. Song of Solomon
2. Daniel (Dan-yell)
3. Proverbs (pro-verbs)
4. Ezra
5. Luke
6. Corinthians (core-in-the-hands)
7. Galatians (Gail-Asians)
8. Titus (tight-us)
9. Genesis (Jenny's sis)
10. Joel (Joe will)
11. Obadiah (O-bed-diet)
12. Mark
13. Jonah
14. Jude ("Hey Jude")
15. Timothy (timid-Thee)
16. Ruth (Babe Ruth)
17. Leviticus (levy-to-kiss)
18. Chronicles
19. Ezekiel (easy-kill)
20. Nahum (neigh-hum)
21. Matthew (book of New Testament)
22. Hosea (hose-ea)
23. James (Jimmy Carter)
24. Hebrews
25. Deuteronomy (due-to-Ron-and-me)
26. Esther
27. Lamentations (lamb-men-day-shuns)
28. Zechariah and Zephaniah (disease = "the Zs")
29. Acts (ax)
30. Thessalonians (the-saloonians)
31. Kings
32. Job
33. Jeremiah
34. Revelation
35. Peter (he denied Christ)
36. Exodus (exit-us)
37. Psalms (in middle of Bible)
38. Isaiah (I-say-ah)
39. Samuel (Sam-mule)
40. Micah (my-cah)
41. John (Johnny Bench)
42. Malachi (mail-a-chi)
43. Romans (Rome-ants) or (romance)
44. Philemon (file-lemon)
45. Joshua (walls of Jericho)
46. Ecclesiastes (Ekkly's siestas)
47. Habakkuk (a-bad-cook)
48. Amos (a-miss)
49. Numbers
50. Judges (give jail sentences)
51. Ephesians (a-fee-shun)
52. Nehemiah (knee-hem-I-ah)
53. Philippians (Flippians)
54. Haggai (Hey, guy!)

Bill Gnegy

BASKETBALL BAFFLER

Here's a game for your hoopball enthusiasts. The object is to identify the NBA teams from the clues on page 76. (Be sure to check this list with a hoopball aficionado—you never know what team moves to what city these days.)

Here are the answers:
1. Portland Trail Blazers
2. Milwaukee Bucks
3. Boston Celtics (cell + tick)

CRAZY BIBLE CLUES

1. A wise king's tune
2. If little Danny lets out a scream, it is a . . .
3. If you are not opposed to words denoting action, you are . . .
4. A captive speaker for the Jews
5. Not actually hot, just _____warm
6. If you are holding the middle of an apple in your palms
7. Two Asian women named Gail
8. Ballerinas wear these on their leg-us
9. Sister to Jennifer
10. Joseph agrees to do something. You could say that...
11. Fifteenth letter + furniture you sleep on + eating only selected foods
12. Right on! You really hit the . . .
13. A whale of a good book
14. Word in the title of a famous Beatles song
15. If a man named "Thee" was shy, he would be a . . .
16. Famous baseball player's last name given to him when he was just a babe
17. A tax on smooching
18. Newspapers
19. A murder that is not difficult
20. The sound of a horse that forgot the words to a song
21. The first of the Bible's new writers
22. You water your grass-ea with a . . .
23. Formal first name of the U. S. president in 1978
24. The Jews, the Israelites, the . . .
25. Ronny and I are collecting an inheritance. We're getting what is . . .
26. A famous swimmer named Williams
27. A young sheep + males + not night + avoids

28. Two answers: Disease of the Old Testament
29. You get this when you're fired
30. The persons born in the old western saloons
31. Higher than Queens
32. An employment
33. A famous bullfrog in a Three Dog Night tune
34. A confusing look at what lies ahead
35. You can't deny this Bible writer
36. When we leave
37. The central book of the Bible
38. The way a shy person might greet a stranger
39. A donkey named Sammy
40. How a person from Brooklyn would introduce his auto. "This is . . . "
41. Formal first name of a Cincinnati Red who rarely sat on the bench
42. If you wanted to ship a Greek letter to someone you might . . .
43. What insects at picnics are called in Italy's chief city
44. What file would you classify a sour yellow fruit in?
45. A successful demolition man
46. When George Ekkly takes naps in Spain
47. Not a good chef
48. Not a hit
49. 6 12 18 43 55 76
50. People who must pronounce their sentences well
51. Refusing to pay a doctor's bill
52. Joint of the leg + make pants shorter + me + sound you make in a dentist's chair
53. Two people born in Flippy, Montana
54. If you're yelling at a strange man from across the room, you might scream . . .

4. New York Knicks (St. Nick)
5. New Jersey Nets
6. Washington Bullets
7. Chicago Bulls
8. Seattle SuperSonics
9. Phoenix Suns
10. Los Angeles Clippers
11. Los Angeles Lakers
12. Philadelphia 76ers
13. Detroit Pistons
14. Sacramento Kings
15. Utah Jazz
16. Cleveland Cavaliers
17. Golden State Warriors
18. Houston Rockets
19. Denver Nuggets
20. Dallas Mavericks
21. Atlanta Hawks
22. San Antonio Spurs
23. Indiana Pacers
24. Orlando Magic
25. Minnesota Timber Wolves
26. Toronto Raptors
27. Miami Heat
28. Charlotte Hornets
29. Vancouver Grizzlies

Tom Daniel

CRAZY QUIZ

Print up the IQ test on page 77 and give your group ten minutes to complete it. Award a prize to anyone who can answer all twenty questions correctly. Exchange papers and give the correct answers. It's good for a few laughs (as well as groans).

Here are the answers:

1. One hour
2. Yes
3. Because he's not dead
4. The match
5. They all do
6. White
7. Halfway. The other half, he's running out.
8. "United States of America" or "In God We Trust"
9. Ten: nine outfielders and a batter; six outs per inning
10. 50¢ and 5¢. One is not a nickel but the other is.
11. Nine
12. Seventy

13. Two
14. No
15. They are sisters
16. None. Noah took the animals, not Moses
17. No. He is dead.
18. Misspelled
19. Whale
20. Damascus

Charles Easley

HIDDEN BOOKS

Print up the story on page 78 and pass it out to your young people. Tell them that there are 19 books of the Bible hidden in the story (one is spelled wrong). The first to find all 19 is the winner.

Answers to Hidden Books:

I once made some re**mark**s about hidden books of the Bible. I was a **lulu!—kept** some people looking hard for f**acts** and studying for **revelation**! They were in a **jam—es**pecially since the books were not capitalized, but the **truth** finally struck **numbers** of our readers. To others it was a hard **job**. We want it to be **a mos**t fascinating few moments for you. Y**es, there** will be some real easy to spot; others may require **judges** to determine. We must admi**t it us**ually takes a minute to find one, and there will be loud **lamentations** when you see how simple it was. One "Jane" says s**he brews** her coffee while she puzzles her brain. Another "**Joe**" looks for a gim-**mick. Ah**, but it can be done by an old **hag**. **Gain** may come slowly, but it's as easy as peeling a bana**na**. **Hum** a tune while you rack your brain with this **chronicle**. Happy hunting!

Dave Bransby

LEADERSHIP TEST

Announce that you are giving a written test (see page 79) to help you determine the leadership potential in the group. Explain that those who are able to follow the test directions are the real leaders of the group. Tell kids to work quickly because of the three-minute time limit. Start everyone on the test at the same time by distributing it face down.

MANGLED MAXIMS

See the list of verbose maxims on page 81. Supply directions that fit your own event and group (for

Basketball Baffler

1. Avenue arsonists _____
2. The money team _____
3. Jailroom bugs _____
4. Santa Claus team _____
5. Fishcatchers _____
6. A shooting team _____
7. The stock market's favorite _____
8. Concorde's crew _____
9. Fireballs _____
10. Hairstylists' team _____
11. Aquamen _____
12. An independent bunch _____
13. Mechanics' men _____
14. A regal team _____
15. Music lovers' favorite _____
16. Gentlemen of the game _____
17. A fighting team _____
18. NASA's favorite _____
19. A golden team _____
20. A free-spirited gang _____
21. High-flying team _____
22. An "encouraging" team _____
23. A step beyond other teams _____
24. The hand-is-quicker-than-the-eye team _____
25. Wood howlers _____
26. Ancient birds of prey _____
27. A steamy team _____
28. An insect team _____
29. The brown bears _____

IQ TEST

1. If you went to bed at 8 o'clock a.m. and set the alarm to get up at 9 o'clock the next morning, how many hours of sleep would you get? _____

2. Does England have a Fourth of July? _____

3. Why can't a man living in Winston-Salem, North Carolina, be buried west of the Mississippi River? _____

4. If you had a match and entered a room in which there were a kerosene lamp, an oil heater, and a wood-burning stove, which would you light first? _____

5. Some months have 30 days, some have 31 days; how many months have 28 days? _____

6. A man built a house with four sides to it and it is rectangular in shape. Each side has a southern exposure. A big bear came wandering by; what color is the bear? _____

7. How far can a dog run into the woods? _____

8. What four words appear on every denomination of U. S. coin? _____

9. What is the minimum number of baseball players on the field during any part of an inning in a regular game? _____ How many outs in an inning? _____

10. I have in my hand two U.S. coins which total 55 cents in value. One is not a nickel. What are the two coins? _____

11. A farmer had 17 sheep; all but nine died. How many does he have left? _____

12. Divide 30 by one-half and add 10. What is the answer? _____

13. Take two apples from three apples and what do you have? _____

14. An archeologist claimed he found some gold coins dated 46 BC. Do you think he did? _____ Explain: _____

15. A woman gives a beggar 50 cents. The woman is the beggar's sister but the beggar is not the woman's brother. How come? _____

16. How many animals of each species did Moses take aboard the ark with him? _____

17. Is it legal in North Carolina for a man to marry his widow's sister? _____ Why? _____

18. What word in this test is mispelled? _____

19. From what animal do we get whale bones? _____

20. Where was Paul going on the road to Damascus? _____

Hidden Books

I once made some remarks about hidden books of the Bible. I was a lulu!—kept some people looking hard for facts and studying for revelation! They were in a jam—especially since the books were not capitalized, but the truth finally struck numbers of our readers. To others it was a hard job. We want it to be a most fascinating few moments for you. Yes, there will be some real easy to spot; others may require judges to determine. We must admit it usually takes a minute to find one, and there will be loud lamentations when you see how simple it was. One "Jane" says she brews her coffee while she puzzles her brain. Another "Joe" looks for a gimmick. Ah, but it can be done by an old hag. Gain may come slowly, but it's as easy as peeling a banana. Hum a tune while you rack your brain with this chronicle. Happy hunting!

Leadership Test

Directions: Answer each question in sequence. If you do not know an answer, go on to the next one. Read through the entire test before answering questions.

1. Print complete name in upper left-hand corner.
2. Print your address here:

3. Underline the correct answer.
    A. A good leader must be: dogmatic, restrictive, dedicated
    B. The best kind of leadership is: authoritative, socialistic, democratic
    C. The best way to get something done is: form a committee, do it yourself, have others do it
4. Put your age in the upper right-hand corner.
5. Raise your left hand until you are recognized by the instructor.
6. True or False (circle correct answer):
    A. A good leader always has an answer. It is a sign of weakness not to have an answer. T F
    B. A good leader should know how to follow directions. T F
    C. A good leader gets things done quickly. T F
    D. It is better to do a job right rather than to do it quickly. T F
7. In question 6B, underline the words *follow directions*.
8. Stand up until you are recognized.
9. Define a leader (approximately 50 words) on the back of this page.
10. If you have read through this entire test as you were instructed to do, you don't have to take it. Just sign your name in the upper right-hand corner and wait until the time is up. Do not answer questions 1 through 9.

example, "In groups of five, figure out the common version of each of the following sayings"), distribute the lists, and have fun! *John E. Morgan*

MANGLED MOTHER GOOSE

Look on page 82 for newspaper headlines that correspond to familiar rhymes. See how many of them your young people can recognize. Set a five-minute limit. Give a prize—perhaps a Mother Goose book—to the winner.

Here are the answers:

1. Little Polly Flinders
2. Peter, Peter, Pumpkin Eater
3. Three Blind Mice
4. Little Miss Muffet
5. Jack Sprat
6. Humpty Dumpty
7. Baa, Baa, Black Sheep
8. Sing a Song of Sixpence
9. Hark, Hark! The Dogs Do Bark!
10. Tom, Tom, the Piper's Son
11. Old King Cole
12. Old Mother Hubbard
13. A Diller, a Dollar, a Ten O'Clock Scholar
14. Pease Porridge Hot
15. Queen of Hearts
16. Rub-A-Dub-Dub
17. To Market, To Market
18. Hey, Diddle, Diddle!
19. Jack and Jill or Ding Dong Bell
20. Mary, Mary, Quite Contrary
21. Jack Be Nimble
22. Georgie Porgie
23. Little Bo-Peep
24. Mary Had a Little Lamb
25. Little Boy Blue
26. Pussy Cat, Pussy Cat
27. Little Jack Horner
28. A Tisket, A Tasket
29. See, Saw, Sacradown
30. This Little Piggy

Doug Newhouse

MIND BLOWERS

The stories on pages 83-84 are great fun at camps and other casual get-togethers to test the group's problem-solving ability. Read each story to the group. The kids become detectives and attempt to solve the problem by asking questions which may be answered "yes" or "no." Solutions are given in parentheses at the end of each story.

To make a contest out of it, have two sharp kids try to solve one of the problems by bringing each kid in one at a time. They ask questions and whoever can get it by asking the fewest questions is the winner. The audience can be clued-in.

Bob Fakkema

MYSTERY BOOKS

Copy the story on page 86 and pass it out to your students. The object is to try and find the 38 books of the Bible hidden in the story. The solution is provided for you in bold type.

Here are the answers:

While motoring in Palestine I met Chief Me**jud, ges**ticulating wildly. His **fez, raiment,** and features were odd. I never saw so di**smal a chie**f. On **market** days he pum**ps alms** from everyone, **a most** common practice. A glance shows that he **acts** queerly. Excuse my spea**king so,** but he was showing a crowd how they used to **revel at Ion**iam bouts, when **the brew** seemed bad.

A fakir was seated o**n a hump**, minus **hose a**nd shirt, and wearing as co**mic a h**at as they make. He pointed **up eternal**ly toward a rudely carved letter **J on a h**igh cliff that was unusually stee**p. "He's,"** I an**s**wered, "absolutely right!"

My companion then cried, "See that **J? Oh,** now I know we are near the Ancient Ai. Is th**is Ai a h**oly place?" **From answ**ers given elsewhere, I'll say not! We asked the age of the

Mangled Maxims

1. Splintered wood and mineral chunks can rupture my skeletal system, but nomenclatures do not impair me.
2. Swab your dentures tri-daily.
3. A needle-and-thread mark in hours passed hoards eight plus one.
4. Do not traverse the gantry until you approach it.
5. Offspring should be endowed with visibility but not oral facilities.
6. Hemoglobin is more viscous in consistency than H_2O.
7. Pulchritude pertains solely to the epidermis.
8. If primary failure is imminent, new attempts should be made repetitiously.
9. The most prompt feathered biped seizes the annelid.
10. Perambulate in moccasins and shoulder a gargantuan wooden rail.
11. Focus your optical apparatus on the spheroid.
12. A maximum of toil and a minimum of disport and dalliance causes Jack to become a dim-witted, stagnant dunce of the young male species.
13. That which is acquired without difficulty is dispersed with equal facility.
14. A red fruit of the Malus genus absorbed into the digestive system every 1440 minutes keeps a medical practitioner from entering the ridge pole of home sweet home.
15. Individuals continuing daily functions surrounded by fused sand structures should be forbidden to hurl missiles.
16. Refrain from enumerating your poultry prior to their emergence from calcified enclosures.
17. A moving and twirling rock picks up no green matter.
18. Departure causes the blood-pumping organ to become more loveable and liked.
19. Distant meadows are inevitably more verdant.
20. Dissipate not needlessly, and impoverishment will not be your destiny.
21. Do not shed tears over a white liquid that has become earthbound.
22. Everything is justified in intense liking and in combat or battle.
23. It is not possible to both retain your angel food or devil's food and consume it.
24. Grab and obtain it, or set it down and release it.
25. View with your optical organs prior to jumping with great steps.
26. A pan under constant scrutiny will never reach 212 degrees F.

Mangled Mother Goose

1. Mother Disciplines Daughter Astraddle Cinders
2. Pumpkin Shell Solves Marital Problems
3. Farmer's Spouse Attacked by Rodents
4. Girl Terrified by Arachnids
5. Married Couple Eat Heartily
6. Men and Mounts Fail To Revive Crash Victim
7. Wool Supply Sufficient, Inquiry Reveals
8. Unique Pie Served to Royalty
9. Dogs Herald Pauper's Appearance
10. Pig Thief Punished
11. Command Performance By Violinists
12. Poverty Strikes Home: Dog Starves
13. Pupil Queried About Tardiness
14. Appreciation of Porridge Varies
15. Tart Thief Repents
16. Scoundrels Bathe Together
17. Swine Sale
18. Animals Display Human Actions
19. Accident Occurs at Well
20. Girl Grows Garden
21. High Jump Skills Displayed
22. Amorous Advances Rejected
23. Lost Lambs Distressing
24. Lamb Incites School Riot
25. Bugler Sleeps on Job
26. Cat Tours London
27. Christmas Pie Reveals Character
28. Multi-Colored Hamper Appealing
29. Directions to London Given
30. Swine Tour, Eat, and Weep

Mind Blowers

Horror Movie

A man took his wife to a horror movie. As he had planned to do, when the audience screamed at a particularly scary point in the show, the man stabbed his wife to death. The noise of the audience muffled any cry from the wife. He took her out the regular exit at the end of the movie, and nothing unusual was noticed by others who were leaving. How did he manage to get her out? (Drive-in movie)

Swiss Alps

A man in New York City read a small article in the paper about a midwestern man who had taken a cruise to Europe with his wife. The article stated that while skiing in the Swiss Alps, the wife had an accident and died. The man in New York immediately phoned the police and told them that he had proof that the woman's death was not an accident. Later that evidence was instrumental in the conviction of the husband for premeditated murder. Who was the man in New York and upon what did he base his action? (Travel agent had sold the man one round-trip ticket and one one-way ticket.)

Guillotine

A man and his wife were sitting on a sofa in the den of their home watching television. He fell asleep in a sitting position with his head bowed. In his sleep, he dreamed that he was in the French Revolution, was captured and imprisoned in the Bastille, and was sentenced to have his head cut off. He was taken to the guillotine and placed in position for the knife to cut off his head. At this point in the dream, the wife noticed he was asleep and hit him on the back of the neck with her fan. He immediately fell over dead. What is wrong with the story? (How would we know what the man dreamed if he never awakened?)

Watchman

Once there was a night watchman who had been caught several times sleeping on the job. The boss issued the final ultimatum and the very next night he was caught again at his desk with his head in his hands, elbows resting on the desk. "Aha, I've caught you again," exclaimed the boss. The watchman's eyes popped open immediately and he knew what had happened. Being a quick thinking man, he said one word before looking up at the boss. The boss apologized profusely and went home. What was the one word? (Amen)

Elevator Ride

Once there was a bachelor who lived on the tenth floor of a luxury apartment building. Each morning he would leave his room, walk down the corridor to the self-service elevator, get on when it arrived, push the first-floor button, ride down, get off, and go to work. Each afternoon he would return to the building, get on the elevator, push the sixth button, ride to the sixth floor, get off, and climb the four flights of stairs to the tenth floor. Each day this procedure would take place. Why? (The man was a midget and couldn't reach beyond the sixth button.)

Hardware Store

A man went into a hardware store and was looking for an item when the clerk walked up and asked, "Yes, sir, may I help you?" "Yes," said the man. "How much are these?" "They are 25 cents each, but you can get 25 for 50 cents and 114 for 75 cents." What were the items? (House numbers)

Elevator Operator

Picture this...it is summertime. You do not have a job. You go downtown and try to get on at numerous places, but find that the positions are all filled. As a last resort, you inquire at an old office building. The manager tells you that he does need an elevator operator and although the salary is small, you take the job because it is the best you can find. Well, everything goes all right for three weeks, and then one day the elevator operator gets a call from the tenth floor. At the tenth floor a 212-pound woman gets on, carrying a 25-pound typewriter and a seven-pound briefcase. The elevator was quite old, and as it moved down past the sixth floor, the cable slipped. You can imagine how frightened they were, but how thankful when the falling elevator slowed down and stopped smoothly at the ground floor. Now, tell me, how old was the elevator operator and what was the elevator operator's mother's maiden name? (Notice the word *you* at the beginning of the story. You, the listener, are the elevator operator.)

One Dead—No Charge

There was a wreck. It was the fault of a man in a small foreign car, who had darted out in front of a big car causing it to crash through a store window. The people in the foreign car were unhurt. In the other car there was one injured and one dead. A manslaughter charge was never filed against the driver of the foreign car. Why? (The big car was a hearse.)

big stone **J.** "**O, el**even centuries at least."

I know that in such a **jam, es**cort was necessary. Besides, our car stuck in a **rut h**ere. So leaving the se**dan, I el**bowed nearer the fakir. A toothless **hag gai**ned access to his side, and paused to **r**est **h**erself on a **mat. The w**oman hinted, "You have treasure?" To which I retorted, "Not **I! Moth, y**ou know, and rust corrupt earthly store!" **Me**j**ud** expressed a wish to accompany us, but I decreed, "Thy party we will not anne**x, O** du**sty** Chief! I am tracing a cargo of lost tobacco. That's my **job**!" To the chief's expression of sorrow over the tobac**co loss I answ**ered, "It would all have gone up in smoke anyway."

My brother is a tram**p (rover), B. S.**, from Harvard, too. His name is Eu**gene. Sist**er is nursing him now. He is still a member of Gamma **Phi. Lemon**ade is his favorite drink when he is ill. They asked, "Where is the prodi**gal at?" I answ**ered that **it us**ed to be incorrect to use "at" that way, but that the **flu ke**pt Eugene at home this year. It really is to**o bad, I, a** homebody, roaming the Orient, and he, a tramp, at home in bed.

Bryan Schoeffler

MYSTERY NAMES

This is like Mystery Books, except this story contains over 80 Bible names rather than books of the Bible. The story doesn't make much sense, but it does include a river, a town, an island, a capital, a large city in Egypt, a valley, a country, a continent, and not less than 77 men and women. Copy "The Rambler" (page 87) and have your group try to find as many names as possible within a given time limit. They can work individually or in teams. You might want to give them a couple of free names just to get them started. Tell them to ignore punctuation marks when looking for the names. The answers appear in bold type, and when two answers overlap, the second is italicized.

Here are the answers:

Major *Dan, I el*ucidate, sang a **solo mon**otonously to the vio**la ban**j**o's eph**emeral strains. "A ra**re hobo am I**," sang he, "who seeks the fount o**f elixi**r of life. I must shun the place where toxi**c ale be**gins to flow." Said he, "I find i**t a bit hard**; I see not **a chanc**e for a **job**. For me this c**risis era** brings hop**e, terror, and despair** alternately. Dia**mon**ds are the **lot** of some, but fate refu**seth** me such things. I have only my ban**jo. Abner** and **Diana, *both*** so well-r**obed** and fed, refuse to help me. In some hotel **I shall** seek what refre**sheth, *ham and* jam** especially. **In cakes there** is delight. I long ago **as a**

pu**pil ate** many in a sing**le visit**. Why should this catastro**phe be** to me? Singing a so**lo is** of no profit. In In**diana** *a man* could find employment and **a habitation**, at least suc**h a man** as I."

So **he rode** a freight tr**ain** to Henry's house. On the door**step** Henry had a **huge, hazily** figured **mat. The w**ork of hemming it was done by his wife. "**Suz*anna,* omit** this **hem**," said **Dan**, "**one hem I,** a handy man, could do evenly if it were well **mark**ed out. This way it mak**es a u**nited pattern."

Henry was hurrying to bring from the **barn a bas**ket of eggs. **Tho mas**sive and strong, he w**as a** *ruthl*ess, parsimo-nious, an**d avid** man with **a grip pa**rticularly strong. He gra**bs a lombard**y popular club, and, **as** *a male k*nave, **put** it us**e**lessly down ag**ain** on the con**cre**te walk, and stood **agog** when he saw who it was. **Dan** with can**dor casu**ally re**mark**ed, "Your wr**ath ensu**es because I **am** ostensibly a stranger. **As I** approached I did not mean to **mar** y**our peace of mind, or **mar that** smile of Sus**anna**'s. I surely do look ra**kish; just usu**al, however." Then playing the ban**jo *as he* r**ose, he stood there and sang a**dept**ly.

"I think the banjo **elegant**," said Sus**anna** *thankf*ully, and she bade him play and sing. He sang a **chor**us, then a ra**cy** *Russi*an folk song, then an **Aramaic** ballad. He had found friends; and now **a big ail**ment, homesickness, was gone.

Bryan Schoeffler

NUMBER NONSENSE

Here are several tricks that are easy and fun to do, but seem baffling to the kids in your youth group and make you appear to be a genius. Try 'em sometime just for fun. It's best to memorize each procedure, and pull them out as if you do it all the time.

• **Choose a Number.** Suggest that someone in your group (or the entire group secretly) choose a number between 10 and 100. This number is not to be told to the leader. He proceeds to find out what the number is. Let's say that the number is 44.

Number selected	44
Double it.	88
Add 1	89
Multiply by 5	445
Add 5	450
Multiply by 10	4500

The leader now subtracts 100 from the result without saying anything. Thus 100 from 4500 is

Mystery Books

While motoring in Palestine I met Chief Mejud, gesticulating wildly. His fez, raiment, and features were odd. I never saw so dismal a chief. On market days he pumps alms from everyone, a most common practice. A glance shows that he acts queerly. Excuse my speaking so, but he was showing a crowd how they used to revel at Ioniam bouts, when the brew seemed bad.

A fakir was seated on a hump, minus hose and shirt, and wearing as comic a hat as they make. He pointed up eternally toward a rudely carved letter J on a high cliff that was unusually steep. "He's," I answered, "absolutely right!"

My companion then cried, "See that J? Oh, now I know we are near the ancient Ai. Is this Ai a holy place?" From answers given elsewhere, I'll say not! We asked the age of the big stone J. "O, eleven centuries at least."

I know that in such a jam, escort was necessary. Besides, our car stuck in a rut here. So leaving the sedan, I elbowed nearer the fakir. A toothless hag gained access to his side, and paused to rest herself on a mat. The woman hinted, "You have treasure?" To which I retorted, "Not I! Moth, you know, and rust corrupt earthly store!" Mejud expressed a wish to accompany us, but I decreed, "Thy party we will not annex, O dusty Chief! I am tracing a cargo of lost tobacco. That's my job!" To the chief's expression of sorrow over the tobacco loss I answered, "It would all have gone up in smoke anyway."

My brother is a tramp (rover), B.S., from Harvard, too. His name is Eugene. Sister is nursing him now. He is still a member of Gamma Phi. Lemonade is his favorite drink when he is ill. They asked, "Where is the prodigal at?" I answered that it used to be incorrect to use "at" that way, but that the flu kept Eugene at home this year. It really is too bad, I, a homebody, roaming the Orient, and he, a tramp, at home in bed.

Books to Find

Acts	Isaiah	Micah
Amos	James	Nahum
Colossians	Job	Obadiah
Daniel	Joel	Peter
Ephesians	John	Philemon
Esther	Jonah	Proverbs
Exodus	Jude	Psalms
Ezra	Judges	Revelation
Galatians	Kings	Romans
Genesis	Luke	Ruth
Haggai	Malachi	Timothy
Hebrew	Mark	Titus
Hosea	Matthew	

The Rambler

Major Dan, I elucidate, sang a solo monotonously to the viola banjo's ephemeral strains. "A rare hobo am I," sang he, "who seeks the fount of elixir of life. I must shun the place where toxic ale begins to flow." Said he, "I find it a bit hard; I see not a chance for a job. For me this crisis era brings hope, terror, and despair alternately. Diamonds are the lot of some, but fate refuseth me such things. I have only my banjo. Abner and Diana, both so well-robed and fed, refuse to help me. In some hotel I shall seek what refresheth, ham and jam especially. In cakes there is delight. I long ago as a pupil ate many in a single visit. Why should this catastrophe be to me? Singing a solo is of no profit. In Indiana a man could find employment and a habitation, at least such a man as I."

So he rode a freight train to Henry's house. On the doorstep Henry had a huge, hazily figured mat. The work of hemming it was done by his wife. "Suzanna, omit this hem," said Dan, "one hem I, a handy man, could do evenly if it were well marked out. This way it makes a united pattern."

Henry was hurrying to bring from the barn a basket of eggs. Tho massive and strong, he was a ruthless, parsimonious, and avid man with a grip particularly strong. He grabs a lombardy popular club, and, as a male knave, put it uselessly down again on the concrete walk, and stood agog when he saw who it was. Dan with candor casually remarked, "Your wrath ensues because I am ostensibly a stranger. As I approached I did not mean to mar your peace of mind, or mar that smile of Susanna's. I surely do look rakish; just usual, however." Then playing the banjo as he rose, he stood there and sang adeptly.

"I think the banjo elegant," said Susanna thankfully, and she bade him play and sing. He sang a chorus, then a racy Russian folk song, then an Aramaic ballad. He had found friends; and now a big ailment, homesickness, was gone.

Names to Find

Abigail	Anna	Dorcas	Joas	Matthew	Seth
Abner	Aramaic	Elisha	Job	Naaman	Shem
Absolom	Asa	Esau	Joel	Naboth	Sheth
Achan	Asher	Esther	Jordan	Naomi	Simon
Achor	Asia	Felix	Joseph	Nathan	Solomon
Adah	Athens	Gad	Justus	Nehemiah	Stephen
Agog	Barnabas	Gehaz	Kish	Obed	Tabitha
Agrippa	Caleb	Ham	Laban	Peter	Thomas
Ahab	Crete	Haman	Levi	Phebe	Titus
Ai	Cyrus	Herod	Lois	Pilate	Uz
Amalek	Dan	Inca	Lot	Put	
Amon	Daniel	Isisera	Mark	Rehoboam	
Amos	David	James	Martha	Russia	
Andde	Diana	Joab	Mary	Ruth	

4400. Strike off the last two digits and announce the number is 44.

• The Age of Your Pocket Change. Have someone in your group think of her age (without telling anyone). Have her double it, then add five, and then multiply by 50. Now add to that number the amount of pocket change someone else has in his pocket. Now have them subtract the number of days in a year—365—from that number. At this point the number can be disclosed to the entire group. To this number you (the leader) secretly add 115. The age of the person will be the first two digits. The amount of change will be indicated by the last two digits.

The person's age	15
Double the person's age	30
Add 5	35
Multiply by 50	1750
Add pocket change (37 cents)	1787
Subtract 365 days in the year	1422
(this number is given to group)	
Secretly add 115	1537

In this example, you announce that the age is 15 and the amount of change is 37 cents.

• When Was I Born? The leader announces that he can guess the age and the month of birth of anybody in the group. He gives the volunteer the following instructions:

Write down the number of the month you were born.

(August)	8
Double it	16
Add 5	21
Multiply by 50	1050
Add your age (16)	1066
Subtract the number of days in a year (365)	701

The leader then calls for the result; he secretly adds 115, making the total 816. He immediately announces August as the month of birth and 16 as the age. The first one or two digits indicate the month and the last two indicate the age.

• Secret Number. This simple trick furnishes fun as the kids try to figure it out. Ask someone to select a number, keeping it a secret. Now ask them to double it, then to multiply by five, and then to tell you the total. Immediately you are able to tell them the secret number. All you have to do is to knock off the

final digit, for what you have really done is to get the number multiplied by 10. Example: The number selected is 13. Multiplied by 2 it is 26. Multiplied by 5 it is 130. Knock off the last digit and it is 13, the secret number. This may be worked on a crowd, the teller staying outside the room while the group decides on the secret number. *Russ Matzke*

PUZZLING PROVERBS

Here's another brain teaser that can be used a variety of ways. Thirty-nine proverbs are on page 90 in abbreviated form. Each line represents a saying in which the key words have been replaced by initials. For example, "The R. to H. is P. with G. I." stands for "The road to hell is paved with good intentions."

You can print up this list in its entirety and pass it out to your group to see who can solve the most proverbs. Or divide into teams and have kids in each group pool their problem-solving abilities. Another approach is to write the abbreviated proverbs on the board one at a time. Teams then try to see who can be first to yell out the correct solution. To adjust the level of difficulty to your group, use more or fewer full words in the clues. For example, "The proof of the pudding is in the eating" could be "The P. of the P. is in the E.", "The P. O. the P. I. I. the E." or "T. P. O. T. P. I. I. T. E."

This game could be tied in with some positive learning by discussing some of these proverbs in light of Scripture and personal experiences.

Here are the answers:

1. You can lead a horse to water, but you can't make him drink.
2. A rolling stone gathers no moss.
3. Oil and water don't mix.
4. A penny saved is a penny earned.
5. Nothing ventured, nothing gained.
6. Early to bed, early to rise, makes a man healthy, wealthy, and wise.
7. The love of money is the root of all evil.
8. A stitch in time saves nine.
9. A watched pot never boils.
10. If at first you don't succeed, try, try again.
11. The squeaky wheel gets the oil.
12. Spare the rod and spoil the child.
13. Seek and ye shall find.
14. He who hesitates is lost.
15. Beauty is only skin deep.

16. Make hay while the sun shines.
17. It's too late to close the barn door after the horse escapes.
18. A city set on a hill cannot be hidden.
19. Necessity is the mother of invention.
20. A friend in need is a friend indeed.
21. A bird in the hand is worth two in the bush.
22. Silence is golden.
23. Children should be seen and not heard.
24. Don't cast your pearls before swine.
25. What's good for the goose is good for the gander.
26. A fool and his money are soon parted.
27. You can't judge a book by its cover.
28. Pretty is as pretty does.
29. Don't count your chickens before they hatch.
30. Cleanliness is next to godliness.
31. Where there's smoke there's fire.
32. Patience is a virtue.
33. Time and tide wait for no man.
34. Don't cry over spilt milk.
35. Still water runs deep.
36. Age is no respecter of persons.
37. Don't put off till tomorrow what you can do today.
38. It's an ill wind that blows no good.
39. People who live in glass houses shouldn't throw stones.

Doug Newhouse and Tommy Baker

QUEEN ANNE'S RIDDLE

This is one of those brainteaser games that's fun at informal get-togethers when there's nothing else to do. The object is to solve the riddle. One person (who knows the answer) starts by giving the first part of the riddle: "It is a queen, but not a king." As soon as a person knows what the secret is, they show this by adding to the riddle, rather than giving away the answer. This keeps the game going until everyone gets it or falls asleep, whichever comes first. The riddle might go something like this: "It is a queen, not a king...yellow, but not blue...green, but not red...a roof, but not a ceiling...a door, but not a window...Jimmy, but not James...a wheel, but not a tire...the moon, but not the sun..."

"It" is any word with a double letter. *John F. Brug*

STRING TIE MYSTERY

Here's a simple little game that you can use to test your group's creativity. Hang two strings from the ceiling so that they dangle approximately one foot from the floor (both strings should be about the same length). The strings should be far enough apart so that, while holding the dangling end of one string, the other string hanging down is about a foot out of reach. Challenge anyone in your group to tie the dangling ends of the strings together with no help from the audience. The only thing that can be used in this task is an ordinary pair of pliers.

How is it done? Simple. Tie the pliers to the end of one of the strings and then swing the string back and forth. Then hold the end of the other string, and when the pliers swing close enough, grab them. Untie the pliers and tie the two strings together.

Dennis Banks

WHAT'S THE MEANING?

A good type of quiz that can be used for fun at parties, socials, or to keep kids busy on a long bus trip is What's the Meaning? You will find four quizzes on pages 92-95. Each combination of letters or numbers represents a well-known saying or tells a story. The object is to decipher each one.

Here are the answers to What's the Meaning:
1. Two fellows after the same girl
2. Legal separation
3. Girl with a million-dollar figure
4. Far away from home
5. Looking backwards
6. Money on the line
7. A week with one day off
8. Forty-niners
9. Nothing after all
10. Tooth decay
11. Five degrees below zero
12. Outnumbered three to one
13. Repaired
14. Right between everything
15. Few and far between
16. One after another
17. Easy on the eyes
18. Keep it under your hat
19. Everything's going up
20. Bad spell of weather
21. World without end
22. Starting off with a bang
23. A couple of sharp operators

Puzzling Proverbs

1. Y. Can L. a H. to W., but Y. can't M. H. D.
2. A R. S. G. no M.
3. O. and W. don't M.
4. A P. S. is a P. E.
5. N. V., N. G.
6. E. to B., E. to R., M. a M. H., W., and W.
7. The L. of M. is the R. of all E.
8. A S. in T. S. 9.
9. A W. P. never B.
10. If at F. Y. don't S., T., T. A.
11. The S. W. gets the O.
12. S. the R. and S. the C.
13. S. and Y. shall F.
14. H. who H. is L.
15. B. is only S. D.
16. M. H. while the S. S.
17. I. too L. to C. the B. D. after the H. E.
18. A C. S. on a H. cannot be H.
19. N. is the M. of I.
20. A F. in N. is a F. I.
21. A B. in the H. is W. 2 in the B.
22. S. is G.
23. C. should be S. and not H.
24. Don't C. Y. P. before S.
25. W. G. for the G. is G. for the G.
26. A F. and H. M. are S. P.
27. Y. C. J. a B. by its C.
28. P. is as P. D.
29. Don't C. Y. C. before T. H.
30. C. is N. to G.
31. W. there's S. there's F.
32. P. is a V.
33. T. and T. W. for no M.
34. Don't C. over S. M.
35. S. W. R. D.
36. A. is no R. of P.
37. Don't P. O. till T. W. Y. can D. T.
38. I. an I. W. that B. N. G.
39. P. who L. in G. H. shouldn't T. S.

24. A new slant on things
25. Wolf in sheep's clothing
26. Tennessee
27. Space ship

Here are the answers to What's the Meaning 2:
1. Double standard
2. Tip-Top shape
3. Crossed eyes
4. Double take
5. Banana split
6. Rough edges
7. Several options
8. French curve
9. Rejoice in the Lord
10. He spoke to them in parables
11. Go down Moses
12. Whosoever believes in me
13. Believe on the Lord Jesus Christ
14. Victory over sin and death
15. Justification by faith
16. Narrow way
17. Sunny

Here are the answers to What's the Meaning 3:
1. Sandbox
2. Man overboard
3. I understand
4. Reading between the lines
5. Long underwear
6. Road crossing
7. Tricycle
8. Downtown
9. Split level
10. Neon light
11. High chair
12. Paradise
13. Touchdown
14. Six feet under ground
15. Mind over matter
16. He's beside himself
17. Backwards glance
18. See-through blouse
19. Double cross

20. Check up
21. Oh gross!
22. Cut off
23. Side by side
24. Look around you
25. Paradox
26. Double date

Here are the answers to What's the Meaning 4:
1A Spreading the gospel
1B Upper room
1C A mess of pottage
1D Frankincense
2A Rightly dividing the word of truth
2B Mixed messages
2C Too much of a good thing
2D Not enough money to cover the check
3A Stretching the truth
3B Smokestack
3C Three-piece suit
3D Eggs over easy
4A Fly in the ointment
4B Sign on the dotted line
4C Sideshow
4D Pie in the sky
5A Feeling under the weather
5B Splitting the difference
5C Fancy footwork
5D To be or not to be
6A Cornering the market
6B Bouncing baby boy
6C Slanting the news
6D Condensed books
7A It's a small world
7B Skinnydipping
7C A bird in the hand equals two in the bush
7D Scrambled eggs
8A That's beside the point
8B Hanging in there
8C Flat tire
8D The end of the game

Angus Emerson, Diane Burgess, Herbert Saunders, J. Russell Matzke, Mary Highlander, and Kay Lindskoog

What's the Meaning

1. GIRL FELLOW FELLOW

2. L E G A L

3. GIRL $1,000,000

4. FAR HOME

5. GNIKOOL

6. **MONEY**

7. SUN., MON., TUES., THURS., FRI., SAT.

8. RRRRRRR
   RRRRRRR
   RRRRRRR
   RRRRRRR
   RRRRRRR
   RRRRRRR
   RRRRRRR

9. A L L O

10. 2th DK

11. 0
    D.D.S.
    LL.D.
    PH.D.
    M.A.
    M.D.

12. O U T
    3 2 1

13. RE RE

14. EVERY RIGHT THING

15. F FAR E FAR W

16. 11

17. EZ
    II

18. YOUR HAT
    KEEP IT

19.   S
         G
         N
         I
         H
         T
         Y
         R
         E
         V
         E

20. WETHER

21. WORL

22. BANGFF

23. BRILLIANT SURGEON
    BRILLIANT SURGEON

24. N
      E
       W
    THINGS

25. WOWOLFOL

26. SSSSSSSSSS C

27. S H I P

What's the Meaning 2

1. STANDARD
STANDARD

2. *TOP* SHAPE

3. X

4. TAKE
TAKE

5. BAN ANA

6. **EDGE**

7. OPTIONS
OPTIONS
OPTIONS

8. PIERRE

9. LOREJOICERD

10. BULL
HE SPOKE TO THEM
BULL

11. MOSES

12. MWHOSOEVER BELIEVESE

13. BELIEVE
LORD JESUS CHRIST

14. VICTORY
―――――――
SIN DEATH

15.
JUSTIFICATION/FAITH

16. WAY

17. E

What's the Meaning 3

1. SAND

2. MAN / BOARD

3. STAND / I

4. R|E|A|D|I|N|G

5. WEAR / LONG

6. R O A D (vertical) ROAD

7. CYCLE / CYCLE / CYCLE

8. T O W N (vertical)

9. LE VEL

10. KNEE / LIGHT

11. CHAIR

12. DICE / DICE

13. T O U C H (vertical)

14. GROUND / FEET / FEET / FEET / FEET / FEET / FEET

15. MIND / MATTER

16. HE'S / HIMSELF

17. ECNALG

18. SECRET (circular)

19. ††

20. K C E H C (vertical)

21. O—144

22. OFF / OII

23. SIDE / SIDE

24. KY O U O / L O

25. DOCTOR / DOCTOR

26. DATE / DATE

	A	B	C	D
1.	g o s p e l	room	pottage	CENFRANKSE
2.	WO RD O F TR UTH	EMSEASSG MEGASSSE SAMEGESS GEMASSES MEASEGSS	a good thing a good thing	MONE ✓
3.	truth	smoke smoke smoke smoke smoke smoke smoke smoke smoke smoke smoke	S UI T	EGGS EASY
4.	OINTFLYMENT	. . . . . SIGN	SHOW (upside down)	SPIEKY
5.	THE WEATHER FEELING	diffe rence	FOOTWORK	BBORNOTBB
6.	MAR KET		NEWS	BOOKS
7.	WORLD	BABYBOY DIPPING IN THERE	HABIRDND = BUTWOSH	GEED (mirrored)
8.	T H A T S, .		TIRE	e

Most of these are fall-guy tricks—jokes played on people, either with or without their knowledge. Remember that this sort of crowd breaker is intended for humor and entertainment, not to tease, mock, or otherwise make fun of the fall guy. If the targets of these stunts are good sports and the leader is skilled and sensitive in performing them, the results are both positive and fun.

BUMPY BRAIN

To perform this stunt, choose one student to be your assistant—and tell her beforehand how the trick is done.

Your group thinks of a number between one and 10; someone in the group whispers the number to your assistant. Announce that you will use your expert skill to tell them the number they chose by feeling the bumps on your assistant's skull.

Place both of your hands on your assistant's head—your thumbs on her jawbones near her ears—and pretend to feel the bumps on her skull for a few seconds. What you're actually feeling, however, is how many times your assistant clenches her jaws, which you can feel with your thumbs. Astound your group by declaring the very number they selected! *Les Christie*

SMELL THE BROOM

You'll need to clue in two of your students—a "smeller" and a "broom holder"—to how this next idea works.

At your meeting one student should brag to the group about his keen sense of smell and volunteer to demonstrate this sense by "smelling out" the spot where a youth group member touches a broom handle.

Have your broom holder hold a broom in both hands, with the handle parallel to the floor. After the smeller leaves the room, ask someone from the audience to touch the broom handle anywhere the volunteer chooses. Call the smeller back into the room to smell the broom handle and detect the spot where the person touched it.

As the smeller moves his nose across the broom handle, he keeps his eyes on the broom holder's feet (she should have shoes on). When the smeller's nose crosses the spot where the broom was touched, the holder moves the toes of one foot up and down very slightly to indicate to the smeller that his nose just crossed the spot that was touched. The smeller, now knowing where the spot is, can point to it and ask if the audience wants to try again.

If the movement is slight enough, it won't be detected and can really stump the crowd. It's a lot of fun. *John W. Fritsche*

ABDUL THE MAGNIFICENT

This is a mind-reading stunt which, when done right, is downright spooky. Give each person a slip of paper and ask them to write a short sentence on it. The slips are then folded, collected, and "Abdul" (who can be dressed appropriately) proceeds to perform the task of reading the sentences to the group without opening the papers.

How is it done? Abdul also puts a slip of paper in the box along with the others, and he puts some kind of identifying mark on his. When the reading starts, he picks one of the slips from the box,

rubs it on his forehead, and offers any sentence as a guess as to what is on the paper. He then looks at the paper, and to his dismay he is wrong, but that will soon be forgotten. He can blame it on the fact that the "spirits" weren't quite right yet, but his next try should be better. It's important not to dwell on this mistake long or to reveal what was actually on the paper guessed incorrectly. Just get rid of it and go on.

Abdul holds another slip of paper to his forehead and repeats the sentence that was actually on the previous paper. After rubbing his forehead, he unfolds this second slip of paper, confirms that he is correct, and asks the person who wrote that sentence to identify it. Everyone is impressed. Another paper is drawn and, again, Abdul repeats the sentence that was on the previous slip. Each time he unfolds a slip of paper to see if he is correct, he is actually learning the next sentence. The important thing is to stay one slip ahead. When he comes to his own slip, which has been held until last, he repeats the sentence on the previous slip, and that takes care of all of them. If this is done smoothly, it will really baffle the group. *Mike Andujar*

ART CLASS

Explain that you are an artist in your spare time and that you're going to create a human painting in front of the group. You'll use people instead of paint to create a forest scene. Ask someone to volunteer to be the babbling brook. He or she steps into the scene and repeatedly says, "Babble, babble, babble." Another volunteer, a rustling tree, stands next to the brook and says, "Rustle, rustle, rustle." Do the same thing with whistling grass and howling wind. Then have someone else be the picture frame that races around everyone else in the scene. Once all the characters are smoothly performing their parts, you say, "And now, ladies and gentlemen, there you have it. The babbling brook, the rustling tree, the whistling grass, the howling wind, and the RUNNING SAP!" Begin the applause yourself.

BUCKET ROULETTE

Display several buckets on a table. Cover them with paper so that the contents can't be seen. Tell your group that one of the buckets contains water and that the others hold rice. Invite three daring volunteers, one at time, to have the bucket of their choice dumped on their heads. The game continues until someone is doused with water.

THE BUCK STOPS HERE

Here's a stunt that almost everyone has to try. Place a dollar bill on the ground and challenge the youths in your group: Anyone who can jump over the dollar bill lengthwise gets to keep the dollar.

There is a catch, however. Before they jump over the bill, they must grab their toes (on both feet), and hold on while they jump over the bill. You should also mention these rules:
1. You must jump forward over the bill.
2. If you fall down in the process of jumping, you are disqualified.
3. Your heels must clear the vertical plane at the end of the bill.

Needless to say, it's impossible to do. You may want to try it yourself, however, before you risk your own money, or you may want to put two bills end-to-end to make it even more difficult. *Tom Stanley*

Egg Walk

Lay eggs all over the floor. Then blindfold a volunteer who must walk across the room without breaking any eggs. However, before the blindfolded player begins, have helpers silently replace all the eggs with unshelled peanuts. Then watch the fun.

Russian Roulette for the Chickenhearted

Color four hard-boiled eggs and one raw egg (total of five) with food coloring. Explain to five volunteers that one of the eggs is raw. They choose the egg that they want broken over their heads. No one can pick up or touch an egg while making a selection. For the best results, have five other volunteers stand behind their assigned partner. At a signal, everyone breaks the eggs simultaneously over the players' heads.

Elephant Pantomime

Have a leader pantomime washing an elephant. She does this while Volunteer One is carefully observing and while Volunteers Two and Three are out of the room. Only the audience, not the volunteers, knows in advance what the pantomime is about. When the leader is finished, Volunteer One performs the same pantomime from memory for Volunteer Two, even if Volunteer One doesn't yet know what the pantomime is about. Then Volunteer Two performs it for Volunteer Three. Enjoy the laughs; then let the volunteers try to guess what they just acted out. The pantomime may have changed drastically by the time Volunteer Two performs it.

To ensure that the leader performs a good pantomime, suggest that she do the following: Pull the elephant in on a rope. Tie the rope to a stake. Dip a rag in a pail and wash the side of the elephant, jumping high to reach the top. Crawl underneath; wash his belly and legs. Go to the front and wash his trunk, inside and out, and wash the elephant's ears as well. While washing under his tail, hold her nose, and generally try to be as creative as possible.

Good Morning, America!

This unique attention-getter is guaranteed to cause a stir. All you need is a video camera...and maybe some strong coffee.

The plan is simple. Just show up at the homes of three or four members of your youth group to interview them on video—at 5:00 a.m.! Ask all sorts of

weird questions like "How many licks does it take to get to the center of a Tootsie Pop?" Interview the person's teddy bear, or try any approach that's spontaneous and funny. Responses from kids so early in the morning are bound to be hilarious.

Here are some guidelines:
• Forewarn the parents. They may think you're crazy, but most parents respond favorably to anything focusing some attention on their child.
• Select young people who will respond appropriately. Shy kids will just hide under the covers.
• Make the most of the moment. Wake them up slowly, and have some fun with them before they become fully conscious.
• Take someone along to help. One of you can interview, and the other can work the camera.
• School days are better than holidays or weekends. They'll have to get up early anyway, and the freshness of the experience will help get the word out at school.
• Don't let the cat out of the bag. The only ones who should know anything about your plans are staff and parents. Surprise is essential.

Show the interviews at a regular meeting, or make the video an attraction for a special event. *Sam Dobrotka*

HOBBY HOAX

Find two or three volunteers who pursue some kind of hobby. Explain that you are going to ask them general questions about their hobbies. They are to respond truthfully but vaguely so that it is not easy for the group to identify their hobbies. To help the contestants relax, ask them a sample question such as, "Where do you work on your hobby?" Give them a chance to answer. Just before dismissing them from the room, explain that the group will quickly come up with more questions as soon as the volunteers leave.

Once the volunteers are out of earshot, tell the others that they are to assume that each hobby is . . . kissing! When the volunteers return and begin to answer questions, the audience will think their answers are hilarious.

Other questions to ask are: How long does it take you to do your hobby? What sound does your hobby make? Is there any special training involved? If so, what? How old were you when you first learned your hobby? When is the best time of day to perform your hobby? What do you wear when you are working on your hobby? What sort of special equipment do you need?

HOMESHOW

One entertaining opener for the topics of home life or lifestyle is a slide show featuring the unmade beds, messy desks, crammed closets, piles of clothes on the floor, and (rarely) neat appearances of the bedrooms of group members. Billed as an insider's view of some of the finest homes in the nation, the show allows the commentator loads of fun as individual shrieks and moans are heard above the general laughter. Taking the slides while the young person isn't home provides an excellent opportunity to visit with the cooperating parents. *David Rasmussen*

IN A JAMB

Just before you are ready to dismiss your group or move to another area for a different activity, extend this challenge to a volunteer: "I say that you can't hold an egg with two fingers for 15 seconds without dropping it." Then have the volunteer extend his or her fingers through the space at the hinge of an open door (between the door and the doorjamb), and place the egg between his two extended fingers. Count off the 15 seconds; then just walk off and leave him there.

PING-PONG FLOUR BLOW

Have two teens compete to see who can be the first to blow a Ping-Pong ball out of a round bowl. After a winner is declared, blindfold the same players and let them try again. Have the loser go first. But just before the original winner takes a turn, dump a cup of flour in the bowl.

SKYDIVING LESSON

Have a volunteer skydiver stand on a sturdy two-foot-by-four-foot plank, which is lifted up by two strong guys. The volunteer can use a leader's shoulder as a brace to keep from falling. After the board is lifted about three feet high, the skydiver tries to jump into the middle of a small circle that you have drawn on the floor. She gets five points for hitting the target. The board is lifted higher, and the skydiver jumps again for 10 points. The last time, for 20 points, the skydiver must jump while blindfolded. However, this time, the skydiver doesn't know that the board has been lowered to just two or three inches from the ground. The leader should stoop low, so that the skydiver thinks she is high. She jumps, but usually falls flat on her face.

SUBMARINE RIDE

A volunteer lays flat on a table with a person standing at each arm and leg. The legs are the left and right rudders. The arms are Torpedo One and Torpedo Two. A jacket is put over the volunteer's head with one sleeve directly on his or her nose. This is the periscope. The captain (a leader) yells, "Left Rudder!" (Person at left leg raises leg.) "Right Rudder!" (Raise right leg.) "Torpedo One!" "Torpedo Two!"(Raise arms.) "Up Periscope!" (Sleeve is lifted straight up.) "Dive! Dive!" (Leader pours water down sleeve and into the volunteer's face.)

SUCTION EXPERIMENT

Announce an interesting scientific demonstration which "will clearly demonstrate laws of gravity, psychology, coloidal suspension, suction, and surface tension." Have ready a ladder or chair which enables you to reach the ceiling, a glass of water, and a broom. Choose a fellow from the group to be your assistant. Lift the glass of water to the ceiling and have your assistant press the broom handle up against the center of the bottom of the glass, holding it against the ceiling. Then climb down and remove the ladder or chair. Point out the "interesting" result of your experiment: "Although suction cannot hold a glass of water to the ceiling, human beings with a broom can do so for a long time." Whether you let him climb up to get the glass down or let him drop it is up to you. *Kathryn Lindskoog*

TAXATION WITHOUT REPRESENTATION

Tell volunteers that you will pay five dollars to anyone who can say "Taxation without representation" 10 times in 10 seconds. This is practically impossible. However, an alert volunteer might figure out the trick: to simply say "taxation" 10 times. That is, in reality, what you want to be said: to say "taxation" without saying "representation." Try it on several kids and see if any can get it.

THERE'S A B'AR!

Get a few kids to line up in a straight line, shoulder to shoulder, with the leader at the right-hand end of the line. All should be facing the audience if the activity is done in front of a group. The leader then says, "There's a b'ar!" (bear) and the kids are instructed to say, "War?" (where) and the leader responds with, "Thar!" and points to a spot off to his left, but with his *right* arm. The kids are instructed to point also, and keep pointing. Again the leader says, "There's a b'ar!" The kids reply, "War?" and the leader says, "Thar!" and this time points to his right with his *left* arm. The kids do the same and now have both arms pointing (crisscrossed). The same things are repeated, this time with the leader squatting and pointing with his left leg to the right. All the kids do the same. Once more the same is repeat-

ed and the kids must point with their noses to the left. So now the kids are turned to the left. The leader then gives the kid next to him a push (while their heads are turned the other way) and the result is that the entire line will fall like dominoes. *John Bristow*

THREAD THE NEEDLE

Find out which player can, with one eye closed, thread a needle in the shortest time. Give the first player a needle and thread, appoint a timekeeper, and to assure that he will only use one eye, put your hand over one of his eyes. Give each player two tries, first using one eye and then the other. Before you put your hand over the last player's eye, secretly smear lipstick on your hand. Then smear it all over her face.

TIPTOE THROUGH THE PASTURE

The "pasture" is set up ahead of time. Get fresh horse or cow manure and scatter plentifully over a specified area. Tell everyone they are going to be blindfolded and led through the pasture. Take everyone off to another area to be blindfolded and they all remove their shoes. While everyone is away, next to the "pasture" place a lot of crumpled, wet paper towels. The kids are led through this, one at a time, and the fancy footwork is fun to watch! After each kid has done it, let him watch the others. *David Brown*

WALK THE PLANK

Place a board on the floor and an obstacle of some sort at the end of the plank. Blindfold a victim who must walk the plank and jump over the obstacle at the end of it. Remove the obstacle before the victim gets to it, so that she jumps over a nonexistent object.

WATER EGGS

Poke a small hole in each end of an egg and empty its contents by either blowing or sucking on one end. Plug one end with wax (paraffin) and fill the egg with water through the other end. Then plug that hole with wax. The result is a water egg. Use your imagination on how to use them.

WHO HIT ME?

Two players lie on the floor (face-up, side-by-side). Cover them with a blanket so that they cannot see. Place a rolled-up newspaper on top of the blanket. The crowd forms a large circle around the players. Someone steps into the center, grabs the paper, hits one of the blindfolded players on the head (easy does it), drops the newspaper back on the blanket, and runs back to the circle. The person who was hit counts to 10, gets out from under the blanket, and tries to guess who hit him. If the victim guesses correctly, the hitter goes under the blanket and play continues.

If and when your accomplice gets under the blanket, he or she will know to play this trick on the unsuspecting victim under the blanket. After you give a prearranged sound signal, your accomplice is to grab the newspaper from the top of the blanket, use it to smack the person next to him, and quickly pull his arm back in under the blanket. It is possible that the victim won't be able to figure out who hit him.

WEIGHT GUESSING CONTEST

Brag that you have an uncanny ability to guess people's weight within two pounds merely by picking them up. Select three volunteers, two of whom you secretly weighed earlier. Have all the volunteers sit on the floor and tuck their arms under their drawn-up knees. First, pick up the volunteers who are in on the joke (one hand under their knees and one hand on their backs to support them). Guess their weights correctly. When you pick up the third volunteer, have an assistant secretly slip a cream pie on the floor underneath the victim. Then drop him onto the pie.

WHOLE GROUP
PARTICIPATION

The entire group gets in on the act with these crowd breakers, warming them up for the meeting to come or simply breaking the ice with a group laugh. Most of these activities involve light competition—and all will give your kids a collective good time.

IF YOU LOVE ME

Someone who has been chosen to be "It" walks up to someone else in the room and says, "If you love me, honey, smile." The second person replies, "I love you, honey, but I just can't smile." However if he or she smiles while responding, that person becomes "It." "It" can't touch the other person but can do almost anything else to get a smile (make faces, dance, etc.).

BABY PICTURE GUESS

Obtain baby pictures of everyone in your group. Try to get slides so that you can project the pictures onto a wall or screen. If only photographs are available, shoot slides from the photos or pay a local photo lab to do it for you. Give everyone in the group a pencil and paper and have the kids try to guess whose baby pictures are projected. (Have kids number their guesses in order so that there is no confusion.) Whoever gets the most correct answers is the winner.

BEST COMIC OF THE WEEK

Ask kids to read the newspaper's comics in the coming week and bring the ones they think are the funniest. At the beginning of the next meeting, allow them to read aloud the comics they've brought. Then ask the group to vote for the best comic strip and post it on the bulletin board. To add an element of competition, explain that the way you will decide which comic strip to post is by how many kids bring in that particular comic strip. If more kids bring in the "Peanuts" strip from Tuesday than any other comic, for instance, those kids and that comic win. The fun, however, is in reading each strip and laughing (or groaning) together. *Mark A. Simone*

CLAPPING TEST

This crowd breaker gets good laughs and involves everyone. Every time you cross your hands (as if you meant to clap but missed), the whole group should clap. If your hands stop midway through the gesture without crossing, the group must not clap. The fun starts when you fake out the group out by not crossing your hands. Vary your pace. Anyone who makes a mistake is out of the game. Continue playing until there's only one person left.

PASS THE TAPE

Have a toaster and a piece of bread on hand. Also obtain wide double-sided tape or masking tape. After you push the bread down into the toaster, the kids pass a foot-long strip of tape around the room. Whoever is holding the tape when the toast pops up (or when the toaster buzzes) puts an unappealing topping on the toast and eats it. Provide pickles, sour cream, Tabasco sauce, olives, sardines etc.

THE CONTAGIOUS GAME

Stand or seat kids in a circle so that all can see each other. One person starts by describing her "ailment." For example, she might say, "My right eye twitches," and so everyone in the group starts twitching their right eye. The next person might say, "My left foot has the jumps" or "I have whooping cough," and everyone must start doing what he says. After a few people share their ailments, everyone should be jumping, twitching, coughing, sneezing, and having a great time. For double laughs, have someone video the action to show later. *Sue Broadhurst*

CARTOON CREATIVITY

Cut out a number of cartoons from magazines and newspapers, remove the captions, and paste them on large sheets of paper, leaving plenty of room at the bottom. Then hang them on the wall of your room and invite the youth group to make up their own captions and write them in the space provided at the bottom. You could offer a prize for best captions or prime the pump by bringing in captions of your own ahead of time. It's a great way to keep the group occupied when they're coming in, milling around, and waiting for things to get started. *Melvin Schroer*

BITE THE ONION

This is a Truth or Consequences type of game. With the group seated in a circle, begin passing around an

onion, "hot potato" style. After a short while the group leader yells, "Stop!" and the person who is holding the onion at that time may be asked a question on any subject by the person who passed the onion. The person with the onion has the right to remain silent, but if he refuses to answer, he must take a bite of the onion. The onion then gets passed around for another round.

Until the teens get warmed up, you might want to allow them a free pass (not requiring a bite of the

onion). And if you have a few youths who absolutely refuse to play, don't force it. Usually everyone wants to play, and there are only a few voluntary bites taken from the onion. Be sure to have a camera ready to catch facial expressions when a bite does get taken. It's a lot of fun. *Malcolm McQueen*

ENDLESS WORD

Have the group form a circle. One person says a word and then counts to five at a moderate speed. Before this person says five, the person to their right has to say another word that begins with the last letter of the word just said. This continues on around the circle until someone is unable to come up with a word before the count of five. Two misses and the person is out of the game. (Or one miss if you have a very large group.) If it's the person's first miss, she starts it again with any word. No one is allowed to repeat a word that has already been spoken. If no one is being eliminated, have them count to five more rapidly. Or if everyone is getting out, have them count to 10 or 15 instead of five. This game can be quite lively, and you'll soon find out who is out to get the person next to them. *Brian Scuffler*

BIRTHDAY GUESS

Have all your students write their birthdays on a sheet of paper. Collect that sheet, then read the birthdays aloud one at a time while your kids try to match birthdays with people. Kids can guess aloud as you read the dates, or else they can do the matching individually on paper. This icebreaker works best with groups of less than 20 people. *Andrew Winters*

NAME THAT PLACE

This game is great for a small group divided into two teams, or for a group split into several teams. Find a book that has pictures of a number of recognizable spots in your city, or go on a photo spree and take some yourself. Once the group

is divided into teams, hold up a picture for them to see. The group that is first to correctly identify the spot wins a point. The team with the most points wins.

If it is too hard for everyone to see the photos, you could photocopy the pictures, or use slides and project them on a large screen. The team that correctly identifies the most pictures in a given amount of time wins.

Make sure that you include a wide variety of photos—some that are easy to identify, like the city hall or the high school, and some that are difficult, like a pond in a certain park or a tree on a street near the church. *Jan Bartley*

GUESS WHAT

Here's a good game to play at the beginning of an event while people are still arriving. You will need to do a little advance preparation by putting the following items in various places around the room: a jar full of small balls or beans, a ribbon hanging from the ceiling, a display of photos of famous (or not so famous) people, a package that you have weighed in advance, a box with something in it, and an assortment of bottles with a different substance in each bottle which gives off an odor. Then give each person a copy of "Count! Measure! Lift! Sniff!" on page 110.

When everyone has had enough time to try to figure out the answers, have them exchange papers while you announce the solutions. You might want to award a prize to whoever gets the most correct, or separate prizes to the winner in each of the various categories. *Mrs. F. S. Richardett*

ADD-A-LETTER

This game works best with a group of 15 or less. Have the group sit in a circle. One person begins to spell a word by saying a single letter. The next person adds another letter, each person attempting to add a letter without completing a word. A person gets a penalty (you can mark on her hand with a felt-tipped pen) whenever she accidentally finishes a word or is forced to say the last letter in a word. A person is out of the game when she gets five penalties. A person can fake a letter when it seems he is forced to finish a word. If the next person thinks he is faking, and doesn't have a word in mind, she can challenge. If she catches the person who is bluffing, the bluffer gets a penalty. If the person challenged

Count! Measure! Lift! Sniff!

(Write the correct answers in the proper blanks.)

#1
How many BALLS are in the jar?

_____

#2
How many inches long is the
RIBBON?

_____ inches

#3
Write the names of the people
in the PICTURES.

1. _____
2. _____
3. _____
4. _____
5. _____

#4
How heavy is the PACKAGE?
_____lbs. _____oz.

#5
What is in the BOX?

_____

#6
Open the BOTTLES. Sniff!
What is in each bottle?

1. _____
2. _____
3. _____
4. _____
5. _____

Keep this paper. The correct answers will be announced.

can give the word he had in mind, then the challenger gets a penalty. The winner is the last person left in the game. All words must be legitimate words, verifiable in a complete dictionary. *Brian Schoeffler*

THIS LITTLE LIGHT

Each person is given a flashlight (or brings one) and a special code (one flash, two flashes, one long and one short flash, etc.). The number of teams desired determines the number of codes. As soon as the codes are assigned, turn out the lights. By flashing their lights at each other in their special codes, the kids are to group together with others of the same code. No talking is allowed. The group that does the best job of getting together is the winner. *Larry Houseman*

SPONTANEOUS POETRY

Break into small groups of seven to 10 and give each group a piece of paper. The first person in the group writes down a word at the top of the paper and passes it to the next person. The second person contemplates the first word, writes another word just below

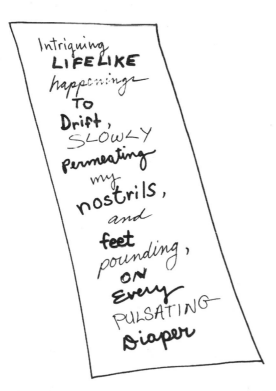

the first word, and then folds the paper so the first word cannot be seen and only his own word is visi-

ble. This process is repeated for each person in the group, with each person carefully folding the paper so that only her own word can be seen. When the last word has been written the paper is unfolded and the "poem" is read.

A person can write any kind of word and should not spend a lot of time thinking of just the "right" word. The results are hilarious. *Richard Pallotta*

REVOLVING STORY

Have kids make up a story or fairy tale as they go along. Each person tells part of the story for 10 or 15 seconds on cue. The results are usually quite funny.

COMMERCIAL TEST

Wrap a dollar bill around any object that can be thrown, such as a tin can, block of wood, chalk eraser, etc. Make a list of commercial slogans, such as, "It just keeps going and going and going," "Just do it," etc. Then toss the dollar to a kid and read one of the slogans. If he can identify the product in five seconds, he gets to keep the dollar. If he can't guess, then he tosses the dollar to someone else and you read another slogan, and so on. The audience must keep quiet (no helping). The dollar is optional. Any prize will do.

FAMILY TIES

Ease students into a discussion of family matters with this crowd breaker. Before the game, list the first names of family members from well-known TV programs, one name per card. Here are some samples:

Cleavers: Ward, June, Wally, and the Beaver
Bradys: Mike (Mr. Brady), Carol (Mrs. Brady), Alice, Greg, Marcia, Peter, Jan, Bobby, Cindy
Jetsons: George, Judy, Jane, Elroy, Astro
Flintstones: Fred, Wilma, Pebbles, Dino

Give each student a card when they enter the room and instruct them to find the other members of their "family." To win, a family must have all its members intact and sing words or hum part of the melody from their "family's" TV program. *Jim Bell*

FOLDING UP

Provide a variety of pieces of paper, square or rectangular. Have at least one for each kid. Include napkins, notebook paper, carbon paper, tissue paper, newspaper, construction paper, onionskin, toilet paper, Kleenex, and paper towels. Make sure there are a few extra-large pieces. Let all the kids choose a piece before they know what the paper is for.

Offer five dollars to anyone who can fold their piece of paper in half nine times or more. (Eight is the absolute limit.) This can be used either as a quick crowd breaker or as an illustration. *Kay Lindskoog*

CULTURE SHOCK

Need a crowd breaker or discussion starter for a teen-parent event? Let them discover how much they know about each other's culture; hand out lists (like the ones here) to the appropriate players (adapt and update your own lists for your group). Instruct participants to get a signature beside each item. *Jim Bell*

Culture Shock

PARENTS: OBTAIN THE SIGNATURE OF A TEENAGER WHO—
_____ Does not listen to (local radio station).
_____ Knows the name of Ward and June Cleaver's son.
_____ Has never used roller blades.
_____ Knows who sang "Go Away, Little Girl."
_____ Believes Michael Jackson really is "history."
_____ Has never been to a drive-in movie.
_____ Thinks Elvis lives.
_____ Reads the newspaper regularly.
_____ Knows Cher's first husband's name.
_____ Thinks school dances are boring.
_____ Eats pizza less than once a week.
_____ Prefers reading to watching TV.
_____ Thinks a girl should never ask a guy out.
_____ Doesn't like Janet Jackson.
_____ Is considering going into the same line of work that a parent is in.
_____ Has never been to Disney World.

TEENS: OBTAIN THE SIGNATURE OF A PARENT WHO—
_____ Used to wear bell bottoms.
_____ Went to school in a one-room schoolhouse.
_____ Knows who sang "Gangsta's Paradise."
_____ Used to grease his hair.
_____ Still greases his hair.
_____ Was an authentic flower child.
_____ Thinks Elvis lives.
_____ Wrecked a parent's car.
_____ Used to have a crew cut or used to iron her hair.
_____ Attended Woodstock.
_____ Wore leisure suits.
_____ Likes to play video games.
_____ Drove a VW bus.
_____ Went to a Beatles concert.
_____ Remembers where they were when President Kennedy was shot.
_____ Liked the Tony Orlando and Dawn show.
_____ Stuck their tongue to a flagpole.

FOOT SIGNING

Have five kids remove their shoes and socks. Give each one a felt-tip or ballpoint pen. On a signal, the five players race through the group to see who can get the most signatures on the bottom of their feet within a time limit. No one person can sign more than three feet. Signatures must be legible.

ETHNIC MIXER

Say, for example, your party carries an Italian dinner theme. As guests enter the room (decorated in green and white and red) and as a violinist plays romantic songs, you hand all guests a questionnaire like the one here that serves as a mixer. Revise the questions to suit your party's theme. Prizes for the first few questionnaires completed could be a jar of spaghetti sauce, a cannoli, or a package of linguine. *Todd Capen*

Ethnic Mixer

1. Find five people in your "Italian Birthday Group," together yell the words printed next to your birthday group, and get the signatures of two people in your group.

X_____

X_____

Italian Birthday Groups:
Jan./Feb./March.
April/May/June.....................................Lasagna! Lasagna! Lasagna!
July/Aug./Sept...Mama mia! Mama mia! Mama mia!
Oct./Nov./Dec..Arrivederci! Arrivederci! Arrivederci!
....Galileo! Galileo! Galileo!

2. Using your most persuasive abilities, ask someone of the opposite sex for a date—and keep asking, until that person screams, "THAT'S AMORE!" Both sign for each other:

X_____

3. On someone else's sheet list the three worst pizza toppings you can imagine:

_____

4. Find someone who could really pass for an Italian. Get his or her signature:

X_____

5. On your own, list four Italian cities:

_____
_____
_____
_____

6. On your own, list three famous Italian buildings:

_____
_____
_____

7. Check the major religion of Italy:
_____ Pedestrianism
_____ Taoism
_____ Yahtzeeism
_____ Bocci Ballism
_____ Roman Catholicism
_____ Rastapastaism

FOR YOUR EYES ONLY

One of the ongoing problems with a youth group meeting is the very beginning—how to keep the interest of the kids who have shown up on time or a bit early, until everyone else has arrived and you can get into the program proper. One way to overcome this is with the memo on page 114, which can be handed out to the kids one at a time as they arrive.

For added atmosphere, seal the memo in an envelope marked CONFIDENTIAL and play some James Bond movie themes in the background. This will keep the kids occupied and running around the church looking for the chocolate bar until it's time for the meeting to start.

Of course, you'll need to hide the chocolate bar

well enough to keep them looking. One suggestion would be to have it in one of the sponsor's pockets, so that the outline of it is in plain view. The lie mentioned in the memo can be anything you want. Be creative. You can adapt this idea any way you like—it works! *Gene Defries*

LETTER SCRAMBLE

Before your next meeting tape a letter of the alphabet to the bottom of every chair in the room. When the group sits down, have everybody get their letter. You call out a word, and the first group of kids to form the word, holding their letter, and standing in order in front of the group, gets a prize. (Your prize can relate to the word you use, such as a package of Certs for the word *halitosis*.)

NAME THAT HYMN

Before your youth group meeting, put together a rhythm band with wooden blocks, maracas, bells, sticks, and so forth. Have the band practice some well-known hymns and choruses using only those instruments. Then at your meeting divide the group into teams and have a contest to see who can guess the hymns as they're played by the rhythm band. It's not easy trying to guess "A Mighty Fortress Is Our God" played on a bike horn or "Away in a Manger" done expertly on sandpaper blocks. *Don Maddox*

FUZZY FOTOS

Collect a number of 35 mm slides of recognizable objects, places, or people. Then show them to your group, but begin by showing them terribly out of focus. Slowly bring each picture into focus and see who can be first to identify the person, place, or thing on the slide.

The secret is in your previewing the slides, carefully choosing those which give odd effects and misleading shapes when out of focus. Cartoons make good choices, as well as pictures from magazine ads. You will also need to practice s-l-o-w-l-y bringing slides into focus in a smooth motion. It's great fun.

Carlita Hunter

HUMAN SCRABBLE

Put one letter of the alphabet on each 3x5 card. Make up enough cards so that you can give each team one-third to one-half of the alphabet plus a few extra vowel cards that you have made up. Give each team 30 seconds to form the longest word possible with the letters they have been given. The team with the longest word wins. Gather up and mix the cards, redistribute them, and play several rounds.

KEY WORD

Explain that you have chosen a key word that you might use in a sentence at any time during the meeting. Choose an unusual word such as *juggler*, *suitcase*, or *candle*. When kids hear the key word, they are to jump to their feet right away. The last person to jump up gets a penalty.

LOVE STORY

Here is a fun crowd breaker that can be used anytime, but would be especially appropriate around Valentine's Day. To begin, you need to have the young people come up with answers to the statements below. The best way to do this would be to pick 17 kids and have each of them respond to one of the statements. Each person should also remember which number they are. Tell them to write down their answers, but not to reveal them until they are asked to do so. Here are the questions:

1. Name a girl in our group.

2. Name a boy in our group.

3. Describe what you were wearing the last time your mother complained about the way you looked.

4. Think of your favorite activity, but do not write that down; instead, name what you were wearing the last time you did this activity.

5. Write down the most useless advice you have ever received.

6. Write down a sentence from the television commercial you most dislike.

7. Name or describe the place you were when you last received some money.

8. Name or describe the worst kind of transportation.

FOR YOUR EYES ONLY!
TOP SECRET!
URGENT!
CONFIDENTIAL!

MISSION:

The FINAL and COMPLETE elimination of zits.

YOUR TASK:

Our government, in conjunction with other governments around the world, has declared TOTAL WAR on zits.

Our department's ongoing task in this vital effort is the total elimination of CHOCOLATE BARS from the face of the earth!

Our intelligence has been able to advise us that a CHOCOLATE BAR has found its way into our church building and is hiding in plain sight somewhere on the main level. We have been able to verify that it definitely is NOT in any of the offices or restrooms.

I want you, personally, to hunt down and DESTROY this fiendish CHOCOLATE BAR, in whatever manner you deem best. You have until exactly 7:43 to achieve this.

Our intelligence was able to determine that if not found by 7:43, the CHOCO-LATE BAR would be turning itself in at the gym, to be DESTROYED by me; therefore, regardless of results, you are to report to the gym NO LATER THAN 7:43:30 for your next assignment.

Oh, one other thing—agent 003 was able to get some vital information to us: With his dying breath, he told us that ONE of the statements listed above is a lie, and is not to be believed. Unfortunately, however, he died before he could give us any further details.

Good luck, 007. Oh, and by the way—you should memorize and destroy this memo.

9. Name or describe what you would least like to be caught doing.

10. Name your favorite food.

11. Name your least liked food.

12. Name or describe the most unusual drink you were ever offered.

13. Name or describe the most unusual thing a person can do on a rainy afternoon.

14. If you were your teacher, what would you have said about the last test paper you handed in? Write this down.

15. Think of the greatest goof you ever made. Write down what you wish you would have said at the time.

16. Name or describe the most annoying habit your brother (or father) has.

17. Name or describe the worst reason a boy could have for breaking up with his girlfriend.

After everyone has an answer, read the story on page 116. The answers to the preceding statements are the missing parts of the story. As you read along, pause at the missing parts, and the person who answered the corresponding question reads what they have written. The results are usually hilarious.

To make this go as smoothly as possible, have all 17 kids (with their answers) get in line according to their number. Then, as you read the story, go down the line and point to the next person whenever you come to a missing section. That person then fills in the blank. *John Bristow*

THE PANTS GAME

Assuming that most everyone wears pants, here's a game for just about any time. Give everyone a score sheet and a pencil, and as you go down the following list, have them award themselves 10 points for each of the following:

• Each pocket
• Each belt loop
• If you're wearing a belt
• If the belt is brown
• If the buckle on the belt is silver
• If there's a Levi tag somewhere on the pants
• If there's ornamental stitching on the pants
• If there are cuffs
• If the hems are frayed
• If there's a grease spot or stain

• If there's a patch
• If there's gold or yellow top stitching
• If there is elastic in the waist
• If there is a wallet in your pocket
• If there is a hole in your pants
• If your pants are any color besides blue
• If your pants are long enough to touch the floor

You can add other things if you wish, possibly including other items of clothing as well. The person who has the highest total number of points is the winner. An appropriate prize might be a patch or an old pair of discarded pants. *Nancy Cheatham*

VOCABULARY TEST

Here's another crowd breaker for parent-teen events. Parents solicit from kids slang words or expressions that their kids use (for example, "she's all . . ." [she said . . .]), and teenagers log in words that their parents' generation used that are strictly dated today

Parent/Student Vocabulary Test

Object: Parents—You are to find out from your teens as many words that they use (for example, she's all . . .) that you would never use.

Teens—You are to find out from your parents words that they used when they were teenagers that are not used today (for example, heavy).

The one to collect the most words will get one free pass to _____.

Name _____

☐ Parent   ☐ Teenager

Word   Definition

1)

2)

3)

4)

5)

6)

7)

(for example, "heavy"). To the teenager who compiles the longest list, award an old Beatles album (or Beach Boys or Herman's Hermits). Give the winning parent a decal or bumper sticker that is fashionable among kids today. *Jack Hawkins*

Love Story

(to be read aloud)

Ladies and gentlemen, we welcome you to another exciting and tearful sequence in the soap opera, "As the World Burns." As you remember, during the previous episodes in the fateful life of our heroine, _____(1), we saw that her one great desire was to have a date with the hero of her youth, the handsome and debonair _____(2). And now the momentous event has become reality for our beloved heroine, for he has indeed asked her for a date! The drama begins as we see him arriving at her doorstep wearing _____(3). As the doorbell rings, she runs breathlessly to answer it, looking her lovely self in her _____(4). As she shyly greets him, her father looks over his evening paper, takes his pipe from his mouth, and says to the newcomer, _____(5). But mother imposes with a tearful _____(6). With this, the couple leave to go to _____(7) by _____(8). Once there, they quickly engage in _____(9). Soon they are hungry, so they go to a nearby restaurant, where each orders _____(10), topped with _____(11), and washed down with _____(12). Afterward, their love deepening as the evening sun spreads its amber glow across the horizon, they decide to end the date by _____(13). As he brings her home again, she lingers on the doorstep, and turning to him with the intense sorrow of parting, speaks these tender words about their time together, _____(14). He, holding back the words he wished he were man enough to say, softly whispers, _____(15). After the date ends, she runs upstairs to her room, her heart beating rapidly, and calls her best friend to tell her the exciting evening events by reporting, _____(16). Meanwhile he walks meditatively off into the rising fog. Tune in again tomorrow, when you will hear him say to his younger brother, after returning from the fog, _____(17).

PUZZLE MIXER

You know that each of your students is important to the group—but do they? Give each one a piece from a jigsaw puzzle (or two or three pieces, depending on the size of your group and the number of puzzle pieces), and give them 30 seconds to find someone whose piece interlocks with theirs. Small prizes may be awarded to those who are successful with this part of the crowd breaker.

Then allow kids 45 seconds to discover as many matches as they can in order to form a large section of the puzzle. The largest group can receive a prize—and all groups see more clearly how, if they want to be involved in the youth group, they must take the initiative. *Michael B. McKay*

QUESTION AND ANSWER GAME

Hand out plain cards and pencils to everyone in the group. Divide into two teams. Have everyone on one team write a question beginning with *how*, such as, "How do you peel a prune?" Everyone on the other team will write an answer beginning with *by*, such as, "By using pinking shears." Collect the cards, keeping them in two separate piles. Read a question first and then an answer. Random reading will produce hilarious results.

SIGNATURES

This mixer can be used with any age group. It's easy and fun to play. Give each person a sheet of paper and a pencil. Written down the left margin of the paper are the letters in a word or phrase selected because of its association with the holiday or the occasion of the party. For example, at a Christmas party, the words written down the side might be *Merry Christmas*.

On a signal the players go around getting the signatures of the other players. They try to find someone whose first or last name begins with one of the letters in the key word or phrase. When someone is found, they are asked to sign next to the appropriate letter. The first person to get signatures next to all of the letters on his or her sheet is the winner. If no winner has come forth after a certain period of time, stop the game, and whoever has the

most signatures is the winner. In case of a tie, first names that match are worth more than last names—so the most matching first names wins. The phrase can be longer for larger groups or shorter for smaller groups. *Lillian Rossow*

S AND T

Divide the group down the middle. Have one side be the S and Ts and the other side be the Everything Elses. The idea is that you will count together as a group from one to 20, and every time you say a number that begins with an *s* or a *t*, the S and T group stands up. On all the other numbers, the Everything Else group stands up. Start slowly, and then do it again a little faster. Each time the Everything Elses stand on "one" and the S and Ts stand on "two and three," and so on. It really gets wild the faster you go.

To make more of a game out of this, have everyone sit in a circle and start counting around the circle, "one, two, three, four, etc." up to 20; then start at one again and so on. Every time a person says a number that begins with an *s* or *t*, they must stand

117

up before saying it. If they don't, they are out of the game, and the game continues. The counting must be done in rhythm without waiting (or the player is eliminated). It's very confusing, but lots of fun. *Sam Walker*

SIT-DOWN GAME

This crowd breaker is always fun and requires little preparation and no props. It involves everyone. Simply have everyone stand up. Announce that you will be reading from a list of "If" statements. If a statement applies to them, they must sit down. Feel free to come up with your own statements in addition to these:

- You didn't use a deodorant today.
- You have worn the same socks for two days.
- Your belly button is an outie.
- You are a girl and have a run in your pantyhose.
- You still suck your thumb.
- You are good looking.
- You hit the snooze button on your alarm clock.
- You watch reruns.
- You have never eaten snail.
- Your mother dresses you.
- You have a hole in your sock.
- You recently got a traffic ticket.
- You are on a diet.
- You have a false tooth.
- You are mad at your boyfriend or girlfriend right now.

End by saying something such as, "Sit down if you are tired of standing;" this will usually get everyone to sit down.

SITUATION GAME

Have players sit in a circle and whisper in the ear of the person to their right "You are ___" and name a celebrity or cartoon character or historical figure. Then have them tell the person to their left "You are ___" and name a place such as "in the bathtub," or "at the White House." Then have all of the kids move to a different seat and tell the person to their right "You are wearing ___." Then have them tell the person to their left "You are ___" and tell them that they are doing something that is crazy or funny. Finally, have all of the players reveal what they were told about themselves—who they are, where they

are, what they are wearing, and what they are doing. For example, someone might say, "My name is Roseanne, I'm wearing a purple bikini, and I'm in a Jacuzzi doing push-ups." If you have a large crowd, have only a few kids tell their story.

SPIDER STOMP

This is a great way to open a meeting. Simply ask your audience to stomp their feet vigorously for 15 seconds. When the time is up, stop them and say, "Thank you. We just wanted to take care of a black widow spider that is loose somewhere in the audience." *Jim Green*

WHY AND BECAUSE

Give everyone in the group a pencil and a 3x5 card. Have them write out a question beginning with the word *why*. Collect them. Now have everyone write out answers on cards that begin with *because*. Collect them. Redistribute them at random and have kids read the questions they received along with the answer. The results will be hilarious. *John Powell*

WORLD'S LARGEST VOLLEYBALL GAME

This is an excellent crowd breaker for large groups seated in normal auditorium fashion (with a center aisle). Simply place a volleyball net (or nets) down the center aisle and toss a large beach-type ball out into the audience. Everyone remains seated and must hit the ball over the net to the other side. Regular volleyball rules prevail, except no one rotates. This is a little difficult to play when you have a low ceiling, but in most cases, it is a winner of a way to involve the whole audience.

WORLD'S LARGEST SOFTBALL GAME

This is similar to the World's Largest Volleyball Game in that you involve your entire audience in the game. Again, you need a center aisle. The pitcher's mound is in the center aisle. The audience is the outfield. Everyone is an outfielder. In a typical audience-versus-staff game, someone from the audience is selected as pitcher and catcher. Home plate is on the stage or platform. The staff is at bat all the time. The pitcher throws the ball (a soft mush-ball or Whiffle ball) over home plate and the batter hits the ball into the audience. The batter then must run to a certain

point and get back to home plate before the audience can get the ball back to the catcher. (Usually the batter runs to the pitcher's mound and back to home, but the pitcher cannot tag him "out" if he gets the ball.) If the batter gets back to home plate before the ball does, the staff gets one point. If he is tagged out by the catcher, the audience gets one point, and so on. When someone catches the ball out in the audience, she stands up and throws it home or relays it up to home. Everyone else remains seated. The batter is not "out" if someone catches a fly ball. Be sure that the ball is nice and soft to prevent damage or injury. Toy stores carry a great foam-rubber ball made especially for indoor use.

PSYCHIATRIST

This indoor game for a small group calls for creativity and encourages kids to get to know one another. Sit the group in a circle and choose someone to be the psychiatrist. The psychiatrist has to leave the room while the game is explained.

Tell the participants that their job is to take on the personality of the person to their left. All questions must be answered as if they were that person. You might want to take one minute and have everyone tell as much as they can about themselves to the person who will be them.

Bring in the psychiatrist. He is free to ask any question he wants and must try to figure out what is ailing these patients. If he begins to notice the pattern, the leader may yell, "Psychiatrist!" and everyone will have to scatter and regroup, taking the identity of the new person on his left. When the psychiatrist can guess what the pattern is, the game is over.

One good variation of this is to have three or four kids leave the room, bring them in one at a time, and see how quickly they figure out the game. Time each one with a stopwatch. The one who figures it out in the least amount of time is the winner.

Scott McLain

Professional Resources

Administration, Publicity, & Fundraising (Ideas Library)

Developing Student Leaders

Equipped to Serve: Volunteer Youth Worker Training Course

Help! I'm a Junior High Youth Worker!

Help! I'm a Sunday School Teacher!

Help! I'm a Volunteer Youth Worker!

How to Expand Your Youth Ministry

How to Speak to Youth...and Keep Them Awake at the Same Time

One Kid at a Time: Reaching Youth through Mentoring

A Youth Ministry Crash Course

The Youth Worker's Handbook to Family Ministry

Youth Ministry Programming

Camps, Retreats, Missions, & Service Ideas (Ideas Library)

Compassionate Kids: Practical Ways to Involve Your Students in Mission and Service

Creative Bible Lessons in John: Encounters with Jesus

Creative Bible Lessons in Romans: Faith on Fire!

Creative Bible Lessons on the Life of Christ

Creative Junior High Programs from A to Z, Vol. 1 (A-M)

Creative Meetings, Bible Lessons, & Worship Ideas (Ideas Library)

Crowd Breakers & Mixers (Ideas Library)

Drama, Skits, & Sketches (Ideas Library)

Drama, Skits, & Sketches 2 (Ideas Library)

Dramatic Pauses

Facing Your Future: Graduating Youth Group with a Faith That Lasts

Games (Ideas Library)

Games 2 (Ideas Library)

Great Fundraising Ideas for Youth Groups

Great Retreats for Youth Groups

Greatest Skits on Earth

Greatest Skits on Earth, Vol. 2

Holiday Ideas (Ideas Library)

Hot Illustrations for Youth Talks

Incredible Questionnaires for Youth Ministry

Junior High Game Nights

Kickstarters: 101 Ingenious Intros to Just about Any Bible Lesson

Memory Makers

More Great Fundraising Ideas for Youth Groups

More Hot Illustrations for Youth Talks

More Junior High Game Nights

Play It Again! More Great Games for Groups

Play It! Great Games for Groups

Special Events (Ideas Library)

Spontaneous Melodramas

Super Sketches for Youth Ministry

Teaching the Bible Creatively

Up Close and Personal: How to Build Community in Your Youth Group

Wild Truth Bible Lessons

Worship Services for Youth Groups

Discussion Starter Resources

Discussion & Lesson Starters (Ideas Library)

Discussion & Lesson Starters 2 (Ideas Library)

4th-6th Grade TalkSheets

Get 'Em Talking

High School TalkSheets

High School TalkSheets: Psalms and Proverbs

Junior High TalkSheets

Junior High TalkSheets: Psalms and Proverbs

Keep 'Em Talking!

More High School TalkSheets

More Junior High TalkSheets

Parent Ministry TalkSheets

What If...? 450 Thought-Provoking Questions to Get Teenagers Talking, Laughing, and Thinking

Would You Rather...? 465 Provocative Questions to Get Teenagers Talking

Clip Art

ArtSource Vol. 1—Fantastic Activities

ArtSource Vol. 2—Borders, Symbols, Holidays, and Attention Getters

ArtSource Vol. 3—Sports

ArtSource Vol. 4—Phrases and Verses

ArtSource Vol. 5—Amazing Oddities and Appalling Images

ArtSource Vol. 6—Spiritual Topics

ArtSource Vol. 7—Variety Pack

ArtSource Vol. 8—Stark Raving Clip Art

ArtSource CD-ROM (contains Vols. 1-7)

Videos

EdgeTV

The Heart of Youth Ministry: A Morning with Mike Yaconelli

Next Time I Fall in Love Video Curriculum

Understanding Your Teenager Video Curriculum

Student Books

Grow For It Journal

Grow For It Journal through the Scriptures

Wild Truth Journal for Junior Highers